**The Proper Care of
Fancy Rats
TW-122**

Photo credits: Glen Axelrod, Dr. Herbert R. Axelrod, Susan Fox, Michael Gilroy, Nick Mays, Lol Middleton, Robert Pearcy, Sally Shore, and Sally Anne Thompson.

Distributed in the UNITED STATES to the Pet Trade by T.F.H. Publications, Inc., One T.F.H. Plaza, Neptune City, NJ 07753; distributed in the UNITED STATES to the Bookstore and Library Trade by National Book Network, Inc. 4720 Boston Way, Lanham MD 20706; in CANADA to the Pet Trade by H & L Pet Supplies Inc., 27 Kingston Crescent, Kitchener, Ontario N2B 2T6; Rolf C. Hagen Ltd., 3225 Sartelon Street, Montreal 382 Quebec; in CANADA to the Book Trade by Macmillan of Canada (A Division of Canada Publishing Corporation), 164 Commander Boulevard, Agincourt, Ontario M1S 3C7; in ENGLAND by T.F.H. Publications, PO Box 15, Waterlooville PO7 6BQ; in AUSTRALIA AND THE SOUTH PACIFIC by T.F.H. (Australia), Pty. Ltd., Box 149, Brookvale 2100 N.S.W., Australia; in NEW ZEALAND by Brooklands Aquarium Ltd., 5 McGiven Drive, New Plymouth, RD1 New Zealand; in the PHILIPPINES by Bio-Research, 5 Lippay Street, San Lorenzo Village, Makati, Rizal; in SOUTH AFRICA by Multipet Pty. Ltd., P.O. Box 35347, Northway, 4065, South Africa. Published by T.F.H. Publications, Inc. Manufactured in the United States of America by T.F.H. Publications, Inc.

The Proper Care of
FANCY RATS

Nick Mays

Dedication

To the enduring memory of Miss Mary Douglas,
the "Mother of the Rat Fancy."

Acknowledgments

My sincere thanks to the following people who have
assisted me so much in getting this book, a long-cherished
personal project, off the ground:

Chris Henwood, Sam Hardy and Karen Brown of T.F.H.
Publications (U.K.); Ann Storey of the National Fancy Rat
Society (N.F.R.S.) for her unrivalled and timely genetical
advice and corrections to the chapter on genetics; The
National Fancy Rat Society for permission to reproduce
their standards of excellence; Gerald and Vicky Coley of
Artis Animal Centre for providing so many rodentine
models for various photographs in this book, plus all the
kind exhibitors at "that" rat show in Sheffield for similar
"model contracts"; Sheridan Smith for her own unique
contributions; my wife Marianne for her patience in
reading my manuscript and for her suggestions on various
points. Last and by no means least, my old friend and
mentor, Geoff Izzard of the N.F.R.S., for soldiering bravely
through the manuscript and writing the foreword!

Contents

About the Author

Nick Mays was born in Mortlake, London in 1962. As a boy, he displayed a keen interest in natural history, although the only pets that he was allowed to keep until the age of 12 were goldfish! His pet-keeping "career" took off when he started keeping salamanders, toads, lizards and numerous other herpetiles. However, he also discovered the charms of somewhat more "regular" pets in the form of gerbils, hamsters and mice.

The turning point came a few weeks after his fifteenth birthday, when he attended his first animal show and discovered fancy rats. It was love at first sight and, although always maintaining a keen interest in all animals, rats were his main love—both as pets and exhibition animals—in the heady world of small livestock fancies. As a member of the National Fancy Rat Society, Nick Mays worked tirelessly to further the "rat cause," occupying many important official positions within the N.F.R.S., including publicity officer, show secretary, and hon. secretary. He became the youngest president of the N.F.R.S. (to date) at the age of 25. He is one of the top fancy rat judges within the fancy.

Also occupying the position of archivist, he pursues his additional interest of researching the history of the rat fancy, and the development of the fancy rat. Nick Mays is a freelance writer for several publications, and a wide variety of subjects, although the mainstay of his work is, of course, related to animals. He is married to fellow fancier Marianne Mays-Bornhult, herself a respected fancier and author. They have one daughter, Rebecca, and live

in Doncaster, Yorkshire, with their extended family of numerous cats, dogs, rabbits, hamsters and, of course, fancy rats.

Nick Mays, the author, is pictured judging at a fancy rat show. Mr. Mays is among the top fancy rat judges in England.

Foreword

It was with some trepidation that I undertook the task of writing this foreword to Nick Mays's excellent treatise on the fancy rat, which, to my knowledge, is the most comprehensive publication devoted solely to this loveable and most intelligent of mammals. I literally dreaded the thought of having to wade through pages and pages of printer's proof. I need not have worried, however, as once I had started I could not put it down.

Anything and everything is covered, and it is a book that is sorely needed by any person who owns a fancy rat or intends keeping one as a pet or breeding one for exhibition purposes.

Personally, I have kept them for nigh on thirty years and congratulate Nick on his research and untiring efforts in producing this work, which deserves unqualified success.

Geoff Izzard
Co-Founder and Life
* President*
National Fancy Rat
* Society*
April, 1992

Introduction

"Rats! They fought the dogs and killed the cats,
And bit the babies in their cradles,
And ate the cheese out of the vats.
And licked the soup from the cook's own sprats,
Made nests in men's Sunday hats,
And even spoiled the women's chats."

Robert Browning
The Pied Piper of Hamelin (1845)

Rats! It's the name really, isn't it? Mention the word "rats" to most people and they'll give an involuntary shudder. Visions of huge, dirty, flea-ridden, plague-carrying rodents, with blazing eyes and razor sharp incisor teeth, swarming out of dank sewers will inevitably spring to mind. Ask most people why rats are to be feared and chances are they'll say that they are vicious, attack people, leap for your throat, eat babies, spread diseases (particularly plague) and gnaw away the very foundations of our homes. If you then proceed to mention that you keep pet rats, most people will back away a little with a look that suggests that you should be placed in a nice padded room in a secure institution somewhere.

Having said all of that, if you then explain that pet rats are really domesticated, or "fancy," rats and totally unlike their wild relatives, most people will hopefully display an open mind and might then even ask to see these fancy rats. Having done so, most rational people will agree that fancy rats are completely unlike wild rats—but they will no doubt still cling to their preconceived ideas about wild rats.

But why the fear? Well, a lot of it is media hype, overstating the problems caused by wild rats in our cities, and towns and in the countryside. Horror movies and fiction play a great part too. If rats are portrayed in either medium, they are usually splashing about in sewers or eating people. Certainly this may *look* convincing, but look closer. Are those rats swimming around the hero really enjoying themselves? Are those rats munching away on the sewer inspector's corpse really eating flesh— or is it peanut butter? In other words, it's all special effects, sensationalism. In fact, the moviemakers would never use *wild* rats; they always use Brown or Black

Profile view of a Pink Eyed White, one of several very well-known fancy rat varieties.

fancy rats. If I received a fee every time I explained that fancy rats are nice creatures, or even that most stories about wild rats are untrue, I'd undoubtedly be a very rich man by now.

Exactly how I personally came to start out on the trail of discovering the charms of fancy rats, I'm not really sure. Like most other children, I grew up with stories about rats and their awesome abilities. Possibly I had more experiences with rats than most other kids— or at least rat-related experiences. I was born and brought up in Mortlake, a suburb of London, in the 1960s. (For a start, Mortlake itself had "ratty" associations. The legend was that when Mortlake was a village outside the city of London, back in the 1300s, bubonic plague victims were shipped out from London and buried in the vicinity, hence the name of Mortlake, "Mort(e)" being the French for "dead." However, that story and the origin of the town's name is open to debate and dispute, but it is an enduring story, especially as rats were carriers of the dread bubonic plague that wiped out a third of the entire population of medieval Europe.) Anyway, like many of the other youngsters down my street, I often used to play down by the river Thames, which flowed quite close by. This stretch of the river was bordered by the huge industrial bulk of Watney's Brewery, and the air reeked of beer. In those days, there was still a fair amount of river traffic for trade, and Watney's used to transport quite a lot of their beer barrels upstream on barges. We used to play by the loading areas, as there were always lots of interesting things to be washed ashore from the then very polluted river. However, we were always wary of rats. Not that we'd ever seen one, but brewery workers used to delight in telling us about "rats as big as cats, which go for your throat if you corner 'em!" One day I found a strange bedraggled furry object washed up by one of the loading bays. At first I thought it was a kitten, as the size was approximately the same. When my friends joined me and we turned the object over with a stick, we all made the shock discovery that it was a rat—or more precisely, a drowned rat. The animal had been dead some time and was a bit decomposed (to say the least from the smell it gave off!). But we could plainly see that it had greyish brown fur, a long naked tail and a fairly broad head with long black whiskers. How the rat had met its fate I will never know, as I later discovered that rats are excellent swimmers, but to my knowledge, that was my first rat encounter. Apart from the possibility that a colony although for some reasons the animals always interested me, never filled me with fear or loathing. Years passed, and my main interest in life began to

A Silver Fawn. This rat has a good, well-shaped head, which would be to its advantage if it were being shown.

of rats lived in an unused outbuilding at my primary school and one or two frequented the back of our garden I never encountered another rat for years, develop further: a love of animals. Never being one to take the easy option, I started with the most exotic species, mainly axolotls, the curious salamander tadpoles that display neoteny and never mature into adult salamanders, plus a smattering of clawed frogs, common toads, green lizards and the like. I always vowed that I'd never go in for "boring furry pets like hamsters and gerbils." Who'd be a philosopher at 11 years of age? By the age of 12 I'd acquired some Mongolian gerbils, which were then relatively new pets. These were followed in rapid succession by hamsters and mice. I think my passing interest in pet rats was started by a reference in an old gerbil book by stating that gerbils were "...not, like *white rats*, born completely tame." Although the statement wasn't entirely correct from the rats' point of view, it was interesting for the fact that the author was referring to white *rats*, so somebody, I reasoned, must keep them as pets. Of course, I knew they were used in laboratories for all sorts of experiments, but as pets?

Then I found some brief references to rats in some of the older books about fancy mice. These references mainly said that rats were basically larger cousins of mice, that fancy rats had been popular for a little while many years ago and that they basically should be fed the same as mice, but more, and housed the same as mice, but in larger cages. All very interesting stuff... but where could one find pet rats? The pet shops never had any.

My interest in fancy mice developed to the stage where I decided to join the National Mouse Club (N.M.C.), which I did in early 1977. I received a handbook from the club, which mentioned various local mouse clubs, one of which really caught my eye: The London & Southern Counties Mouse Club, established in 1915. What was more remarkable was that they held shows each month in Richmond, Surrey—just two miles from Mortlake! Needless to say, I

A nicely coated fancy rat.

hastily contacted the secretary, a very helpful young man named Eric Jukes. During our first telephone conversation, Eric explained that the next show would be held at Richmond Community Centre, their regular venue, in April. However, this show was a special one, for the London & Southern were entertaining the parent club, the N.M.C., for the Spring Cup Show. He then mentioned, almost in passing, that the club also staged classes for fancy rats. This fired my interest even more—I simply had to attend that show! So, on Saturday, 23 April, 1977 I went to my first-ever show—and what a marvellous event it was. I quickly found out that, nice though my fancy mice were, they were nowhere near as good as those being exhibited at the show; I had a lot to learn. After spending quite some time speaking to several mouse fanciers and enquiring about stock for sale, I literally stumbled across the rat section. There weren't many rats on display—or many rat fanciers in attendance, come to think of it—but I was completely taken aback by the truly beautiful animals on display. Whereas the mice were shown in little green wooden cages called Maxey cages, stuffed full of hay to keep them warm, the rats were shown in small plastic fish tanks, with sliding wire mesh lids. There were some white rats there, to be sure, but there were quite a few other varieties also; several strikingly attractive orange-coloured rats, some Blacks, some Browns (which were almost like wild rats, I

thought, but obviously much friendlier) and some curious bi-coloured specimens, with white body fur and coloured heads, with a coloured stripe extending down the spine. In time, I was to discover the names of each variety I saw (Silver Fawn, Black Berkshire, Agouti and Hooded), but on that day I could only marvel at these lovely animals. Could these be the same as the wild creatures that infested sewers? The same species as the drowned specimen that I found in the river, all those years before? Again, I was to learn that although they were the same species as wild rats, they were completely different in all other respects.

The other discovery that I made on that fateful day was that, apart from the classes put on for rats at shows staged by the London & Southern Counties Mouse Club, there was, in fact, a separate specialist club purely for fancy rats: the

National Fancy Rat Society.
I duly joined the society,
paying the vast sum of 50p
for a juvenile membership.
Going to that first show was
truly one of those special
events that change lives...
and my life certainly
changed on that day. Ahead
of me, did I but know it, lay
the joys of keeping, breeding
and exhibiting fancy rats,
travelling to shows all over
the country, meeting
likeminded people, holding
several officers' positions
over the years on the
N.F.R.S. Committee,
learning to judge rats, even
travelling abroad to judge at
shows staged by other, as
then unformed, rat societies.
I would research the long
and varied history of the rat
fancy. My love of rats would
one day lead to my meeting
the other love of my life,
Marianne, my future wife, at
a rat show. Plus, of course,
writing this book... All that
lay ahead of me. I
purchased my first three
fancy rats that day, a Silver
Fawn Rex buck, a Silver

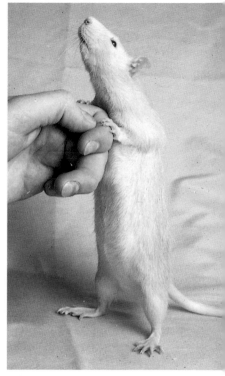

A Silver Fawn. Can you see the
line of demarcation between the
top coat and the pure white belly?

Fawn doe and a Silver Fawn
Hooded doe. (I had
prepared a large cage at
home on the offchance that I
might make such a
purchase!) I actually

Getting acquainted. Rats can make ideal pets for people of all ages.

I think it is a reasonable assumption on my part, Dear Reader, to say that you have picked this book up and read thus far because you are interested in rats. Perhaps you are contemplating keeping some pet rats; perhaps you already have one or two and may wish to learn more, maybe progress to showing them. Maybe you already exhibit them very well and are reading my humble offerings to see whether you agree or disagree with my methods of caring for fancy rats. Whatever your reason for reading this book, you share two things in common with other rat lovers everywhere. The first is a deep interest in a unique animal. The second is an open mind, which has enabled you to look beyond the myth at the reality that is, quite simply, the fancy rat.

purchased them from the co-founder of the N.F.R.S., Geoff Izzard, who was to become a life-long friend in the years ahead, as well as my mentor and confidante in the fancy. It was truly a remarkable day and I had, after several years, at last acquired some pet fancy rats.

Happy ratting!
Nick Mays
Doncaster, 1992

Meet the Rat

"I venture to hope that we shall not have destroyed the rat, an animal of considerable enterprise which has as good a chance as any other of evolving toward intelligence."

J.B.S. Haldanc (1932)

There can be few other animals as misunderstood, or about whom so many inaccurate stories abound, as the rat. For centuries Man has fought a seemingly never-ending war against this incredibly resilient

A pet rat can be very responsive to its owner, particularly if it is handled frequently.

rodent, which has accompanied Man wherever he has gone—but seldom by invitation.

In order to fully understand the fancy rat, it is desirable to learn a little about the pet variety's distant wild cousins and ancestors. Like all other domesticated animals, rats have their roots in the wild. Rats belong to the order Rodentia, the rodents, the most ancient mammalian order to inhabit this planet, originating some 70 million years ago toward the end of the Cretaceous period, the close of the age of the dinosaurs. This order accounts for around 40 percent of all mammalian species. Within the order Rodentia itself, over 1,700 different species have been classified to date. All rodents are characterised by their chisel-like incisor teeth, which are used to great effect for gnawing. In fact, the name "rodent" is derived from the latin verb *rodere*, "to gnaw."

Rats are, without doubt, the most intelligent of the rodents and the most widespread. They are *commensal* animals, which means literally "to share our table," which is what rats have been doing for hundreds, if not thousands, of years. There are many different species of rat worldwide, but the two most common species are in the genus *Rattus*. These are: *Rattus rattus*, the Black (or ship) rat, and *Rattus norvegicus*, the Brown (or Norway) rat. Both species originated in Asia many centuries ago and quickly spread across the known world by a combination of migratory instincts and Man's own ships, when trade and exploration first began.

The two species, although related and sharing many similar characteristics, do have some noticeable,

Opposite page: Rats' ancestors traveled the world aboard ships, often climbing up the ropes—like this agile fellow.

fundamental differences. *Rattus rattus*, the Black rat, as its common name suggests, is predominantly black in colouration, but there are several subspecies with a wide range of colour variations, such as grey-brown, tawny and even pale fawn specimens, some sporting dark dorsal stripes or white bellies. Certain subspecies in India and parts of Asia live an arboreal existence and are often referred to locally as "tree rats" and "roof rats." In general, however, the Black rat is coloured black or very dark brown, with a pointed muzzle, large hairless ears and a long whiplash tail, which is longer than the rat's body and head combined. This rat measures between 14 and 16 inches (35 to 40 cms) in length, is very slender in build and attains a maximum weight of 7 to 8 ounces (200 to 225 grams).

Rattus norvegicus, the Brown rat, is much larger than the Black rat. Again, although as its common name suggests, the colour is predominantly brown, there are a range of variations. Albino and Black individuals can occur naturally, although in the wild they would stand very little chance of survival. It was through colour mutations that fancy rats originated during the 1800s. The Brown rat has a blunter muzzle than the Black, small furry ears, and a tail that varies in length, reaching a maximum length of the body and half the head combined. General size ranges between 14 and 18 inches (35 to 45 cms).

Both species are omnivorous scavengers, having a wide-ranging diet. This includes corn, wheat and other cereal crops, both growing in fields and stored in barns, birds' eggs, insects, carrion, fruit, vegetables and human refuse. In short, just about anything that's edible. Rats have a well defined colony structure and forage in

A Chocolate rat. In the wild, rats are pests that can cause considerable damage to their surroundings.

packs, although occasionally, certain individuals live alone in burrows. They are prolific breeders, reproducing at quite a staggering rate, especially under ideal weather and feeding conditions. The female rat may produce five litters in a year, each containing an average of eight kittens (or pups, as they are sometimes called), although litters as large as sixteen have been recorded in wild colonies. One of the many fallacies about rats is that they are very cannibalistic toward their offspring, although in reality such traits are confined to sickly litters, or when a source of food abruptly ceases. Generally, cannibalism extends only toward old or sick members of a colony who cannot contribute effectively to the well-being of all. Rats are, in fact, very protective of their offspring. If danger threatens, both the doe and buck will carry the kittens to safety.

Rats communicate with each other by a series of high-pitched squeaks and low grunts, inaudible to the human ear. There is a definite "pecking order" in colonies, with rats asserting their dominance by a series of bodily postures and stances, as well as the ability to fight any challengers with devastating effect.

Certainly rats have a high level of intelligence in relation to their size. This, coupled with their reproductive abilities, makes each species a formidable enemy to mankind. Every year, rats cause untold millions of pounds worth of damage to stored foodstuffs, buildings and drainage

A day-old rat kitten—born blind, deaf, and naked. The average litter size of a female rat generally numbers around eight.

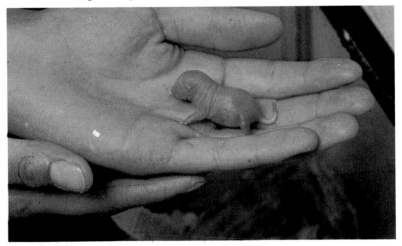

systems. Several fires have been caused by rats' gnawing through electrical cables and wires, and even lead gas pipes. As a result of this widescale damage, Man has waged war on the rat over the years with ever increasing ingenuity. Poisons, of course, form the mainstay of rat control, but the rat's strong bodily constitution and rapid adaptability have allowed it to build up a resistance to most poisons within a very few generations. Poisons such as warfarin, created specifically to eradicate rats, have very little effect nowadays. In fact, there are recorded instances of rats being observed to eat the poison with relish! More sophisticated methods of rat control have had to be developed. When it was discovered that rats communicate by high-frequency squeals, ultrasound devices were developed and placed near known rat burrows and in sewers, etc. For a time, it

Rats are very agile animals. They can easily make their way into a myriad of nooks and crannies.

appeared that the high-frequency, abrasive sounds emitted by these new devices had greatly helped in containing the rat problem—or at least in moving a colony of rats out of one area and presumably into another!

Rats are known to possess a condition known as *neophobia*, a fear of new things. In this way, they are extremely cautious and avoid many traps and devices placed in their carefully-marked-out foraging routes. This neophobia, coupled with their learning ability, makes extermination very difficult. Black and Brown rats may be contained, but never totally eradicated.

FACT AND FICTION

Many stories—indeed legends—have grown up around rats over the centuries. Stories abound of rats eating people alive, stripping grown men down to the bone, attacking babies and the like. Horror fiction writers and moviemakers have used rats in this misguided context for many years, reinforcing the horrific rat legends. It must be admitted, though, that the legends contain a grain of truth. Rats *do* swarm, usually in the spring or autumn, leaving their burrows and hideaways. But the swarming occurs only if there is a population explosion, in which case

A Champagne rat. Throughout the centuries, the rat has been the subject of many notorious myths and legends.

Rats are curious but cautious when it comes to investigating new things. Thus, they often avoid traps and similar devices with ease.

they collectively swarm to seek new quarters, or indeed if circumstances in a given area drastically change, thereby forcing the rats to seek new territory. In Europe, such swarms—often termed "plagues"—have been documented, although accounts of many have been greatly embellished over the years. One well documented and relatively accurate account concerns a swarm of many hundreds, possibly thousands, of Brown rats swimming across the mighty Volga river from Asia into Europe. The swarm had apparently been caused by a terrible earthquake, which forced the Brown rats to seek new territory. This has led to the theory that this was the event that caused the Brown rat to enter Europe and thereby displace

One of the most famous rat-related legends is that of the Pied Piper, who mysteriously rid the town of Hamelin of rats.

recorded in Europe prior to this event.

Of course, the most famous legend concerning a swarm of rats is that of the Pied Piper, who rid the German town of Hamelin of a particularly bad infestation of rats in the year 1284. Apparently he played a melody on his flute which "charmed" all the rats into following him out of the town and into the river Weser, whereupon they all drowned. The mayor of Hamelin, however, reneged on the deal struck with the Piper and did not pay him for his incredible services, which led the Piper to employ the same method on the town's children and lead them all away into the Koppelburg Mountains. The story is an old one, and most accounts are nowadays influenced by Robert Browning's famous poem on this event. Closer scrutiny shows that much of the story is just that—a story, with even the date, 1284, being suspect. But

the Black rats already resident there, although both species had been once again, truth lies somewhere within the legend; possibly Hamelin *did* suffer from a plague of rats that *may* have been passing through. The famous Piper, clad in his bright two-tone costume (hence *Pied* Piper) could be any one of several characters involved in the events. What is extremely interesting is the use of a pipe to attract the rats—an early use of ultrasound, perhaps? Who can say? It's a great story, at any rate.

Swarms of rats still occur. In recent years, with the wild rat population on the increase because of milder winters and excessive rubbish mounting up in British streets, the U.K. has seen quite a number of mass migrations of rats. As to rats attacking people and stripping their flesh to the bone, this too, is doubtful. True, if a person were to lay down in the path of a swarm of rats, he might lose a few fingers in the process, but people seldom undertake this exercise to prove a

A pair of pet rats contentedly perching on their keeper's shoulder.

point. Rats have, however, on occasion been reported to eat human corpses in crypts and uncovered graves; in such cases the bones are consumed as well as the flesh. Babies *have* been bitten in their cots by marauding rats, but such instances are rare nowadays except in poor areas of the world, where there is little protection against predation by rats.

As for "rats as big as cats," no rat ever achieves a size of more than a feline kitten. Certain related rodent species such as the coypu and capybara do reach such proportions, but certainly not the Black or the Brown rat.

Finally, the most enduring legend of all: that a cornered rat will leap for one's throat. A rat, if cornered, will not really want to fight—certainly not with a creature much bigger than itself. In such a case, the rat will use its powerful hind legs to spring toward the largest expanse of light that its poor eyesight can perceive, and this usually will be over the person's shoulders.

KING RAT OR RAT KING?

Another story that never seems to die and which, in fact, has grown in strength in recent years, largely thanks to horror fiction and movies, is that of the "king rat." This remarkable animal is said to be the result of chemical or radioactive contamination, which has altered its body and brain cells to the extent that a mutant species of "super rats" has evolved, the leader of which—the "king" (or sometimes even queen) rat—controls, directing foraging operations, which no doubt include the capture of as many human babies as possible. An intriguing story, to be sure, and maybe not totally beyond the realms of some sort of possibility, but certainly not a proven fact. The "king rat" story tends to get mixed up with the "rat king" story. Rat kings, however, are a definite fact. There are many documented and photographed cases of "kings"—groups of up to 12 rats, all joined together by their tails, which are tied up in an inextricable knot! These kings are sometimes discovered alive, although

A Pink Eyed White. Given the fact that rats are hardy and resourceful, it is not surprising that they have survived throughout history—even under the most adverse of circumstances.

often all or some of the rats within the "king" are dead or dying. Any live specimens captured thus far have always ended up dead after discovery, at any rate. A recent and very celebrated king was discovered by a farmer in Rucphen, Holland, in February 1963. The king consisted of five does and two bucks, all of similar age and size and all appearing to be well fed and healthy (up until the time the farmer killed them, of course). The king was sent for scientific analysis, and various tests were conducted. X-ray photographs showed that the tails of the rats had been knotted for some considerable time and that some of the caudal vertebrae (tail bones) had begun to atrophy. None of the bones were fused together, however, thus ruling out any notion that the rats were all littermates and had been born forming some sort of "Siamese septuplet." There was no evidence either to suggest that the tails had been knotted together by human hands. Basically, the end result has been the same for all kings discovered over the centuries: there is no adequate or clear-cut explanation as to how the rats become joined together in this fashion. Nor is any explanation forthcoming on why the phenomena are confined to *Rattus rattus* only. Despite many theories put forward over the years, to this day the case of the rat king remains a mystery—a real rat enigma.

HISTORY AND DISTRIBUTION

Until relatively recently, the "official" history of the rat and its distribution, largely from an Anglo-Saxon point of view, was that the Black rat "colonized" England and other western European countries by being brought back on ships containing Crusaders returning from the Holy Land between the years 1095 and 1191. After

If cared for properly, a pet rat can be a truly delightful little pet.

several centuries of spreading bubonic plague, the Black rat was usurped by the larger and more adaptable Brown rat around the beginning of the eighteenth century. However, fresh evidence suggests that rats of both species were pretty well distributed and established in many countries well before the Middle Ages.

Bones of Black rats dating from at least the third century A.D. have been unearthed in archaeological excavations in Britain and Sweden. It is extremely likely that Black rats were distributed throughout the world by stowing away on Roman ships. After all, the Roman Empire covered a vast area of the known world—why should rats not have become established elsewhere in this way? Why wait until the relatively few Crusaders' ships journeyed back from the Middle East, a rather limited voyage area?

A Hooded rat preparing to snack on a tidbit.

Sanitation and public hygiene were unknown when the Black rat began its incursions into Europe. With an abundance of rotting food, raw sewage and other unsavoury articles in the streets of villages, towns and cities, the rats began to thrive. Also to the Black rat's advantage, nearly all houses were constructed out of wood—extremely easy to gnaw into. With human diseases such as dysentery and diphtheria being commonplace and therefore weakening people's resistance to any other diseases, it was inevitable that an epidemic such as the dreaded bubonic plague should take hold and have such a devastating effect. For many years it was unknown that rats actually helped to spread the plague, although in 1896 such a link was discovered by scientists investigating the bacterium. The bacterium itself is carried in the stomach of the flea *Xenopsylla cheopis*, which in turn lives in the rat's fur and feeds by sucking blood from its host. An infected flea is unable to suck blood easily, and therefore gets very hungry. At this stage the canny flea will transfer to another host—either a rat or human being—and attempt to suck blood from the new host. In doing so, infected blood from the flea's stomach is regurgitated through its needle-like mouth parts and into the victim's bloodstream. After a variable incubation period, the bacterium takes hold in the victim's body, causing large swellings, particularly under the armpits and in the groin region. These swellings are called *buboes*, hence bubonic plague.

The Plague—often termed the Black Death—devastated Europe in the Middle Ages. It is estimated that over a third of the entire population of Europe was wiped out, causing society to break down and undermining the whole fabric of life as it was then. The Plague hit Britain several times over the centuries, sometimes isolated outbreaks causing a few deaths in a limited range, sometimes causing thousands of deaths. The worst outbreaks were in the years 1348, 1361, and—

Rats have poor eyesight but highly developed senses of smell and hearing. Their whiskers aid them greatly in detecting distance.

most often recounted of all— 1665. This latter outbreak was extremely virulent in large towns and cities, as population levels had grown tremendously in urban districts in previous decades. London suffered abominably that year, with many contemporary drawings and engravings showing handcarts piled high with plague-ridden corpses being transported out of the city for burial in mass graves in outlying districts. Samuel Pepys, the famous diarist, recorded the passage of the plague throughout 1665 and 1666 in London. The culmination of this was, of course, the Great Fire of London in 1666, which scoured the plague from the city at least. (Interestingly, the Great Fire caused only six recorded human fatalities.) An interesting aside to all of this is that certain evidence has come to light that suggests that some of the outbreaks of plague may not have been the bubonic plague at all, but possibly smallpox, for which, at the time, there was no known cure. So, in some way, *Rattus rattus* may be exonerated as a plague carrier, *perhaps*. The last recorded British outbreak was in Glasgow, Scotland, in 1900, again being prevalent in slum conditions.

THE BROWN RAT COMETH

Rattus norvegicus, the Brown rat, began its steady colonisation of Europe in the early eighteenth century. Exactly *why* it gained such a foothold is not completely clear, but one suggestion is that house building styles had changed, with stone being more widely used. Brown rats, being bigger and stronger, were able to burrow into the stronger structures much more easily than Black rats. Also, sewer systems were being built around this time and the adaptable Brown rat was able to make a home in such damp and squalid conditions, whereas its Black relative could not thrive in such an environment. Like the Black rat before it, the Brown rat travelled into different countries by ships, as world trade had increased tremendously. Britain was one of the first countries to be "colonised," probably because of its vast trade fleet. The Brown rat certainly arrived in Britain around 1714, at the same time of the arrival of the highly unpopular Hanoverian King, George I. People recognised the incursions of the new breed of rat, so political jokes linked the rat with the hated monarch, which led to it acquiring the nick-name of the "Hanoverian rat" for some time. In fact, some stories alluded to rat and king arriving in England on the same ship! The adaptable invader multiplied, quickly colonising fields, barns, sewers and cellars. Wherever it met the indigenous population of Black rats, it would drive these out or fight and kill them. For a period of time around the mid-eighteenth century, Brown and Black rats did exist in roughly equal numbers. An account written by Princess Amelia's

A Pink Eyed rat in a stance that is typical of rats and other rodents as well. Note how the bottom claws are spread to help maintain balance.

Royal Ratcatcher around 1768 details how, in many houses that he visited to ply his trade of rodent extermination, the Black rats tended to occupy the upper levels and attics, which were warmer and

A Black Eyed White Rex. This variety is among one of the newer ones in the rat fancy.

drier, whilst the Brown rats lived in the colder, damper cellars and basements. He also noticed that, if ever Brown and Black met, the Brown would attack and kill the Black. The Royal Ratcatcher wrote of one particular incident:

"I set all my traps ... as usual and in the lower part of the house in the cellars I caught the Norway rats (sic), but in the upper part of the house I took nothing but Black rats. I then put them in a great cage together to keep them alive till the morning, that the gentleman (the householder) might see them, when the Norway rats killed the Black rats immediately and devoured them in my presence."

Eventually, the Brown rat became the dominant species, and for many years it was assumed by science that the Black rat was completely extinct in Britain. However, in the late 1890s it was discovered that a few colonies did still exist, and it was, in fact, a later rat fancier who brought them to prominence. To this day, Black rats are confined to small colonies in certain docks and ports, and a few rural areas, where the Brown rat has not established a permanent foothold. Colonies of both Black and Brown rats exist side by side on the island of Lundy, in the Bristol channel. The Brown rat spread across the globe rapidly, reaching France and Italy by 1750, Norway by 1762 (giving lie to the misapplied name of "Norway rat" in other countries), Sweden by 1790, and Spain by 1800. It was gaining prominence in the United States of America in the 1760s, mainly due to the large number of immigrants coming into the country from Europe.

RATS AND SCIENCE

Exactly when laboratory rats were developed for use in all manner of scientific experimentation is a matter

Scientific experimentation and research on rats has been extremely useful to man. This is especially true in the field of medicine.

for conjecture. One of the earliest strains of laboratory rats was developed in the Wistar Institute, Philadelphia, U.S.A. in 1906. Laboratory-bred rats are predominantly Albino or Hooded-pattern "domestic" versions of the Brown rat. However, it is said that the Black rat was originally used in crude scientific experiments in the Scientific Renaissance in the 1660s. However, the Brown rat is a versatile and hardy species, ideal for all manner of scientific tests. Its physiology closely resembles Man's in certain respects, so therefore the bulk of scientific tests are of a medical nature. No matter what moral arguments may be directed against medical experimentation on rats—or indeed any animal— particularly nowadays when so many alternatives to live animals are available, it is a fact that rats have been instrumental in many key areas of research into many terrible diseases. Rats also figure highly in psychological experiments, including the effects of modern day stress to the brain, behavioural and learning techniques. Rats even helped pioneer the early space program, with one such celebrated rodent astronaut being "Hector," a national hero in France. In 1961 he "piloted" an early

space rocket for several kilometres into the lower atmosphere.

Finally, however, science has some surprising facts about rats as a species, which we would do well to consider. It concerns rats' possibly becoming the next dominant species on this planet. Evidence for this dates back to the late 1940s and early 1950s, when the U.S. Navy was conducting a series of atomic bomb tests in the Eniwetok Atoll in the Pacific Ocean. One island, named Engebi, was pounded again and again by atomic bombs, leaving the island cratered, barren and devoid of all plant or animal life ... or so the scientists conducting the tests thought. When scientists visited the island in 1950, they made two discoveries. The remaining plant life and soil were highly radioactive—just as expected. The other discovery was far more mind-blowing. Dr. William B. Jackson, a scientific task

An Agouti rat. This colouration is sometimes referred to as the wild-type colour because it is exhibited by numerous types of animals in the wild.

force leader recounted how "... The island abounded with rats. Not maimed or genetically deformed creatures, but robust rodents so in tune with their environment that their lifespans were longer than average. The rats' burrows shielded them from some direct effects of the blasts, but any way you look at it, their survival was uncanny." This leads to the quite possible scenario that if ever mankind was destroyed in whatever manner, that rats would slip into the niche left vacant by the dominant species on Earth. Whether they would evolve into creatures such as ourselves, who can say? However, the fact remains that rats have existed for thousands of years and show every sign of continuing to do so for some considerable time yet... and maybe even longer than us!

Fancy Rats and the Rat Fancy

"Are rats getting a fair deal?"—Geoff Izzard & Joan Pearce, *Fur & Feather*, January 1976

The fancy rat is, undoubtedly, an animal of great charm and intelligence. It is highly attractive, being bred in an increasingly wide range of colours and patterned varieties. Its popularity as a pet has grown rapidly over the years, as has its value as an exhibition animal. Nowadays, very few eyelids are batted by pet lovers or fanciers when rats are mentioned as ideal pets.

ORIGINS

Of course, the fancy rat didn't just appear overnight. Like the development of all domesticated species, this process took time. Also, as with so many other animal domestications, it is not at all clear exactly when rats were first domesticated. Mary Douglas, the first great rat fancier, once stated that the first Albino rats were introduced into Great Britain by a travelling entertainer from France, around the year 1800. However, it is likely that "domesticated" rats were in existence long before that, given mankind's aptitude for capturing all manner of animals over the centuries and developing them, for practical use in various forms and even to worship. Rats, too, have been deified by mankind! Even today, in parts of India and Pakistan, rats are venerated in temples to various deities, who were once said to have appeared in the form of rats. The temple rats, usually *Rattus rattus*, are given free

Fancy rats are attractive, intelligent, tame, and clean. What more could you ask for in a pet?

Exhibitors checking over their rats as a show gets underway.

and rat, rather akin to the ancient Egyptians' veneration of the cat, again said to be the earthly form of the goddess Bast.

In Victorian times, wild rats were captured in the hundreds, particularly in London, and sold for use in "rat pits"—a far cry from being venerated as gods! A rat pit was an enclosure, usually in the basement of a public house, where men of all classes and social status would go to watch dogs, usually terriers, kill the unfortunate rats, which were dropped into the pit. Large sums of money changed hands in bets over which dog could despatch the largest number of rats in the shortest time. Generally, the terrified rats would cower in a corner of the pit, huddled in a large mass of bodies, whereupon the dogs would leap into the huddle and tear the rats to pieces. In fact, in their day, a number of dogs earned quite formidable reputations as "ratters," and, as such,

run of an area of the temple, and pilgrims are invited to buy food to feed to the rats. Although these rats aren't "domesticated" in the strictest sense of the word, they are the closest ancient example of a respectful association between Man

A fancy rat clambering about the top of its cage. If you don't want your pet to do this, make sure its cage is latched securely.

gained a lot of monetary value for their owners. One such dog was "Billy," who was said to be capable of killing 100 rats in just five minutes. At the height of this barbaric sport's popularity, there were over 40 known rat pits in London alone.

Despite the appeal of "ratting," some domesticated rats were bred and sold as pets in the period between the 1840s and 1860s. Two men are known to have bred and sold domesticated rats and may truly be credited as the originators of fancy rats. Both are mentioned and quoted at length in volume three of the greatest sociological study of Victorian life in London, *London Labour and the London Poor*, published in 1861 by Henry Mayhew. Mayhew literally walked hundreds of miles in London, interviewing all manner of ordinary people and recording their observations on life in the capital city of the greatest empire in the world. In many cases, life was extremely harsh and unfair to Mayhew's subjects, and the publication of his *magnus opus* led to a great deal of social reform. The two men in question were both associated with wild rats by way of their professions. The first, Jimmy Shaw, was a publican, managing one of the largest sporting public houses in London. Shaw was a dog fancier of some note, and many of his patrons who flocked to his rat pit brought along dogs bred by Shaw, to engage in some ratting. The interview given to Mayhew by Shaw is largely concerned with wild rats and the sport of ratting, but a most interesting paragraph concludes the interview:

"After finishing his statement, the landlord showed me some very curious specimens of tame rats—some piebald, and others white, with pink eyes, which he kept in cages in his sitting room. He... handled them without the least fear... the little tame creatures did not once attempt to bite him.

In one of these boxes, a black and a white rat were confined together, and the proprietor... remarked, "I hope they'll breed, for though white rats are very scarce, only occurring in fact by a freak of nature, I fancy I

A Hooded rat. Rats are known for their proclivity to gnaw, and items such as wicker will be readily shredded to bits.

shall be able... to breed 'em myself... The first white rat as I heard of came out of a burial ground. At one time I bred rats very largely, but now I leaves that fancy to my boys, for I've as much as I can do continuing to serve my worthy patrons."

Presumably, Jimmy Shaw sold these rats (as pets) to anybody who wanted them, although this fact is not recorded by Mayhew. However, from the lengthy section devoted to Mayhew's second interviewee, it is noted that domesticated rats *were* bred and sold as pets sometime during this period. The originator of the first, true domestic rats was, by profession, a rat catcher. Jack Black was no less than official Rat Catcher and Mole Destroyer to Her Majesty, Queen Victoria. To say that Jack Black was a character would be to greatly understate the man himself. Black even designed himself a uniform consisting of a tall black hat, scarlet waistcoat, a long green velvet coat and a belt across his shoulder, inlaid with cast-iron rats. As Black himself said, "I used to make a first-rate appearance, such as was becoming to the uniform of the Queen's rat-ketcher (sic)." Needless to say, he was a well-known figure in the metropolis, often to be seen plunging his hands into cages of wild rats and holding several of the rats

A young Champagne Rex. This variety is distinguished by its curly coat, which in this youngster is especially well developed.

aloft for the crowd to see, but without sustaining any bites in the process. Naturally, during the course of his long career, he did suffer many, many painful rat bites, at least two of which were near fatal, laying him up for several weeks at a time. Black sold his own "Rat Bite Composition" to anybody who was fearful of being bitten, a useful supplement to his government payment and his regular contracts for rat-catching work. He also supplemented his income by supplying many captured wild rats to several rat pits, including Jimmy Shaw's (where he once saved Shaw's son Bob from a very nasty mauling by a ferret). However, during the course of his rat-catching activities, he noticed certain specimens with unusual colours—natural mutations—as sometimes occur in many species of animal. The colours included Albinos and Blacks, even Fawns and

Pet rats can make interesting and amusing pets.

Greys. He kept several of these and bred them together, developing coloured and patterned offspring, which he sold as pets. Black is quoted at great length by Mayhew. Of pet rats, he says:

> "I've bred the finest collection of pied rats which has ever been knowed in the world...

over eleven hundred of them... I've sent to all parts of the globe, and near every town in England. When I sold em off, three hundred of them went to France. I ketched the first white rat I had at Hampstead and the black ones at Messrs Hodges and Lowman's in Regent Street, and I bred them in. I have 'em fawn and white, black and white, brown and white, red and white, blue-black and white, black-white and red... They got very tame and you could do anything with them. I've sold many to young ladies for keeping in squirrel cages."

Although Jack Black did, undoubtedly, exaggerate much of what he told Mayhew, as befitting the showman he was, his rat breeding, in the main, sounds entirely plausible.

A little later than the time that Jack Black was plying his trade, the famous children's author Beatrix Potter, famed for her stories of *Peter Rabbit, Squirrel Nutkin*, et al., was a young girl, growing up in London. She had a pet white rat herself at this time, named "Sammy." In fact, when her book *Samuel Whiskers*, the story of a very unsavoury wild rat and his wife, Martha, was published in 1908, she dedicated the book to her pet rat Sammy, naming him as "The intelligent pink-eyed representative of a persecuted (but irrepressible) race, an affectionate little friend and most accomplished thief." Could her rat Sammy have been a descendant of Jack Black's own "pied rats"? It would be nice to think so. Further literary evidence for domesticated rats can be found in Howard Spring's novel *Fame Is The Spur*, which tells the story of the working class's struggle through the eyes of various characters from the 1860s to the 1930s. In the early part of the story, the young heroes Hamer Shawcross and Arnie Ryerson collect scrap metal to sell to local businessman Tom (later Sir Thomas) Hannaway, who trades white rats for any decent items of scrap metal.

THE RAT FANCY

So, as we have seen, domesticated rats were not so uncommon in the latter part of the nineteenth century. It was, therefore, an almost natural step from their being mere curiosities and children's pets to

An inquisitive Pink Eyed White resting securely in the confines of its owner's hand.

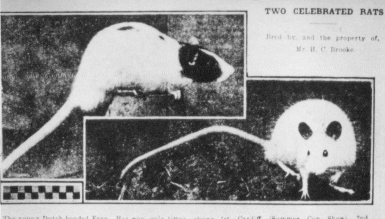

TWO CELEBRATED RATS

Bred by, and the property of, Mr. H. C. Brooke.

The young Dutch-headed Even. Has won, only times shown 1st Cardiff (Summer Cup Show), 2nd Bristol, 2nd Maidenhead, 1st Gloucester, N M & E C Annual, also Medal second best Rat. The Cream. Rattus Rattus, is one of that strain, now fixed by Mr. Brooke, which is exciting the interest of naturalists all over the world. Has won (only times shown) 1st Cardiff, 1st Bristol, 1st Douglas Cup, and Silver Medal N M & E C Annual, Gloucester. He is as tame as any Fancy Rat. The photos are by Miss Frances Pitt.

A page from the January 1922 issue of *Fur & Feather*. Shown are two top show rats of the day, both bred by top fancier H. C. Brooke. One is a *Rattus norvegicus*; the other is one of Brooke's celebrated Black Eyed White *Rattus rattus* specimens.

desirable exhibition animals. Of course, as with the development of the fancy rats themselves, the organised rat fancy didn't just happen; it developed gradually. In fact, it grew out of the mouse fancy, so that is where we must pick up the story...

Mice had been steadily rising in popularity as exhibition livestock in fancy circles since the early 1890s, when several articles were penned about them and their care by interested fanciers in the fanciers' magazine *Fur & Feather*, which catered to cats, rabbits, cage birds, poultry, pigeons and cavies. The culmination of this interest was that in 1895 a group of

The rat fancy has come a long way since its beginning at the end of the nineteenth century. There are more fanciers than ever—as well as more color varieties of rat.

mouse fanciers founded the National Mouse Club.

The club really took off when a young man named Walter Maxey was appointed as the second Hon. Secretary in 1897, a post which he was to hold for ten years. During the ensuing years, the number of members in the club grew, and many successful shows were staged. It was largely as a result of Maxey's devotion that the fancy prospered so quickly, and it was also thanks to his foresight that fancy rats were catered to by the N.M.C. It all came about in early 1901, when a Miss Mary Douglas wrote to Walter Maxey asking whether the N.M.C. would

Miss Mary Douglas, the legendary "Mother of the Rat Fancy," pictured with one of her beloved animals. She served as Hon. Secretary of the National Mouse and Rat Club on three separate periods and later became president of that esteemed organization.

consider "opening its doors" to the larger cousins of mice, namely rats. Thanks to Maxey's help, the N.M.C. Committee agreed that rats be admitted. The first-ever classes for fancy rats were staged at the Aylesbury Town Show on October 24, 1901. Miss Douglas's "black and white even marked" (the forerunner to today's

Some would-be rat owners looking over stock for sale at a rat show in England.

Hooded variety), won Best In Show against several others entered. Things progressed speedily for rats from then onwards, with several rat fanciers joining the N.M.C 's ranks. Although there were never as many rat fanciers as mouse fanciers, fancy rats were bred in a vast range of different varieties, and often the rats were of a superior type and size to the mice shown. However, fancy rats in those days were not as tame and tractable as today's specimens. In those days, fanciers thought nothing of capturing wild rats and crossing them into their fancy stock to improve size and type. There were several instances of judges' being bitten by rats—something that would not be tolerated nowadays! Mary

Douglas must take much of the credit for the rise in rats' popularity in those days. As Walter Maxey was later known as the "Father of the Mouse Fancy," so Miss Douglas became known as the "Mother of the Rat Fancy." Like Jack Black, Miss Douglas was a larger-than-life character, a real English eccentric. For a start, there was her love of rats—unusual enough for someone from a privileged background. Her father Henry Douglas was at one time Dean of Worcester Cathedral, himself the second son of the Earl of Morton. It was from him that Mary inherited her income (she described herself as "a spinster of independent means") and her Christian values. Much of her time was devoted to charitable pursuits, especially for animals. Indeed, during the First World War, she organised special shows for the animal charity The Blue Cross, in aid of injured war horses on the Western Front.

Undoubtedly, she had a very strange, but striking, appearance, as her photographs bear out. She was very masculine in both appearance and dress. Apparently, in her hometown of Lostwithiel, in Cornwall, she would often drive a pony and trap into town, clad in breeches, leggings and a wide straw hat, often puffing away on a clay pipe!

Miss Douglas's efforts for the good of the rat fancy are legendary. She wrote numerous articles about rats and their care for *Fur & Feather* over a twenty-year period, her most enduring and famous column being "Rat Resume." By the 1912 annual general meeting, there was enough support "rat-wise" within the club for a motion to amend its name to be carried by a large majority. Thus, the club became known as the National Mouse *and Rat* Club. Although, undoubtedly, rats were her

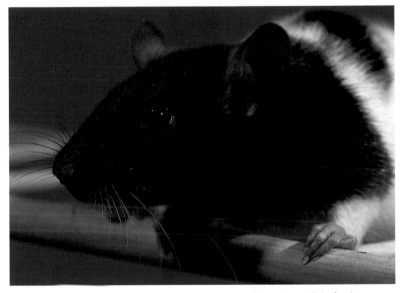

A typically alert fancy rat. Because of the configuration of their claws, rats are adept at grasping and holding on to things.

greatest "fancy passion," she worked actively for the good of the club as a whole. She took over as Hon. Secretary when Walter Maxey stepped down in 1907. In all, she held this post on three separate periods, and later became president—a high honour, indeed. Amongst Miss Douglas's cherished beliefs was that the future of every fancy lay amongst its junior members, so, for many years, she conducted the "Junior Fanciers" column within *Fur & Feather*. She was so highly respected by fanciers in all fancies that she was able to successfully pioneer a plan whereby established fanciers would actually donate good stock to youngsters who wished to "take up" the fancy seriously. Miss Douglas made several such donations herself, often anonymously, as indeed she donated a great number of trophies for award at N.M.R.C. shows. During the twenty-year period from 1901 to 1921, the rat fancy grew alongside the mouse fancy, with the establishment of several regional and specialist mouse and rat clubs. However, from 1918, just after the First World War, the rat fancy began to decline markedly, largely due to the fact that Miss Douglas was ill and couldn't attend as many shows or write the same volume of rat articles. In this respect, the strength of the rat fancy truly made it a "one-man" (or one-woman) show, as so many rat fanciers appeared to be apathetic. There was one happy exception to this situation—Ralph Blake, a young and enthusiastic, highly intelligent fancier. He succeeded Miss Douglas as "rat champion" following her sad death in 1921 at the age of sixty-five. Blake must also take much of the credit for keeping the rat fancy going and, indeed, restoring it to something of its former glory by "whipping up" rat fanciers via long and detailed articles in *Fur & Feather*," in his position as new Hon. Secretary for the N.M.R.C.

During this period, varieties such as the popular Silver Fawn were developed, with "Even Markeds" becoming better known as "Japanese" or "Hooded." Around this time, a well-known scientific animal expert, H.C. Brooke, one of the pioneers of the still-new science of genetics, developed fancy strains of *Rattus rattus*. It had been believed that all the Black rats had been driven from Britain by the Brown rat, although a few isolated colonies were discovered. Brooke didn't see any reason why Black rats shouldn't be developed for exhibition purposes as had

Brown rats, and to some extent he was successful, although *Rattus rattus* never proved to be as popular as *Rattus norvegicus* amongst fanciers (the former being rather more timid and less tractable). However, Brooke Ralph Blake and H.C. Brooke. Therefore, things looked bleak again when, in 1923, Blake left the fancy to take up duties as manager of a large rabbit farm in Sussex. One of the pre-conditions of this excellent

The fancier of today can choose from a wide variety of attractive colors and patterns. In fact, he may find it difficult to select just one!

managed to develop Black Eyed White, Fawn and even exotic Greenish specimens during the early 1920s!

Again, however, the rat side of the N.M.R.C. was largely left in the hands of a very few stalwarts such as job was that he give up all publicity for the "long-tail fancy" (although why, I can't fathom. After all, the mouse and rat fancy hardly interfered with the rabbit and cavy fancies). Blake took up his position and, in later years, emerged as a highly regarded judge and exhibitor of rabbits. The rat cause was then taken up by a Mr. William Turton, who bred a great many winning rats, especially Hoodeds. Turton was also an accomplished fancier of mice, and was one of the few fanciers to make his hobby truly pay. One issue of *Fur & Feather* carried his photograph on the front page with the banner headline: "This Man Makes £100 a Year From Mice." In those days, £100 was a tremendous sum of money. Sadly, though, support from other ratters dwindled, Turton moved onto mice, and the rat fancy was, effectively, dead. The great slump of the late '20s and early '30s hit hard against all fancies and fanciers, particularly the mouse and rat fancy. There were far too many area and specialist clubs, the N.M.R.C. was nearly in debt, and things were in disarray. Eventually, all the clubs agreed to disband and re-form within the parent group, which once again was to "weather the storm." Thus, in 1929, the big re-organisation came about and the club became the *National Mouse Club*, with the words "and rat" dropped from the title. In 1931, support for rats was formally dropped altogether, although there was still provision within the club rules and constitution for rats to be catered for, should they ever regain their popularity.

In the mid to late 1930s, a Mr. D. Tuck tried to re-kindle interest in rats via advertisements in *Fur & Feather*, proudly proclaiming that he had the largest collection of fancy rats in his commercial mouse and rat farm in Essex. However, the response from any ratters was predictable—nil. Occasionally, one or two rats would be shown at large shows, whenever any classes were laid on for them—usually one or two at

An aquarium can make an ideal home for your rat.

the most—but then only as "curiosities," never as serious exhibition animals. Any such specimens were always *Rattus norvegicus*, all fancy specimens of *Rattus rattus* having long since died out.

Needless to say, most of the varieties of fancy rat had died out and the fancy was, well and truly, dead. Even rare articles in *Fur & Feather* in the 1940s failed to elicit any response. The year 1957 proved to be a turning point. This was the year that some sharp-eyed individual noticed that rats were still catered for in the N.M.C rules, so it was voted to drop all references to rats from the rules and constitution. However, that same year, this short-sightedness was offset by an orchestrated revival of the rat fancy. A group of fanciers from the South Coast of England started writing articles about rats in *Fur & Feather*, and this time some interest was generated. These fanciers, Eddie Gay, Derek Rayfield, Frank Pink, and Mrs. Jean Curzon, succeeded in getting some rat classes staged at that year's Portsmouth Town Show. A good number of rats were entered and shown. In response to this, the London & Southern Counties Mouse Club reinstated their rat classes, having dropped them many years previously. Articles continued to be written about rats in *Fur & Feather*, leading to more rat classes at the 1958 Portsmouth Show. However, the rat entry was noticeably lower, interest clearly flagged, and, once again, fancy rats went into a period of decline.

Compared to many other pets, rats have very simple requirements. Proper housing, a good diet, and fresh water are the three basic elements of good rat care.

Another revival came about a few years later in 1962, when a young Welsh fancier named Ron Philips founded the *National Fancy Rat Club*, a fact that was proudly proclaimed in *Fur & Feather* on June 7, 1962. A few interested fanciers joined up, and some articles were written and published in *Fur & Feather*. Sadly, however, interest in this first-ever specialist club for fancy rats fizzled out. The club had ceased to exist by 1963—without ever having staged a show.

Apart from the occasional "curiosity" rat entry at shows staged by the London & Southern Counties Mouse Club, the next few years were again very bleak rat-wise. It was the L&SCMC Secretary Eric Jukes who tried to start a new rat club in 1969. Jukes wrote a series about fancy rats for *Fur & Feather*, entitled "Origins and History Of The Fancy Rat," in the hope of whetting the appetites of would-be ratters. In 1969, he wrote an article in the N.M.C. yearbook, proclaiming that 1969 would be "The Year Of The Rat," and outlined his plans for the new *International Fancy Rat Council.* Alas, again insufficient interest put paid to any "rat revival." Undeterred, Jukes tried again in 1970, by proposing at the N.M.C. annual general meeting that the N.M.C. should cater for and promote fancy rats for a probationary period of five years. Although many fanciers backed the motion, it failed to gain the two-thirds majority necessary to get rats back into the N.M.C. rules. Then, when all seemed lost for fancy rats, the old maxim of "Third Time Lucky" came into play...

Geoff Izzard, a herpetologist (reptile and amphibian specialist), had kept rats for many years, initially to feed to snakes and the like, which he kept and imported as a sideline. However, over the years, he had become very interested in fancy rats in their own right, particularly since he had given his young

A Dark Eyed Champagne. This attractive variety is somewhat lighter than its relative, the Dove.

daughter one as a pet. Of particular interest to Izzard were the few colours and patterned varieties in which rats were available, and he wanted to know more. Thus it was, with the help of his old friend Albert Collins and other contacts in the mouse fancy, that he exhibited some rats at the prestigious London Championship Show in 1974, in the hope of attracting like-minded people. Although some visitors to the show were interested, the exercise met with limited success. However, upon leaving the show, Izzard missed his bus and had to wait at the bus stop for about half an hour. He was joined at the bus stop by Mrs. Joan Pearce, a teacher. Mrs. Pearce noticed the rats in the cages on Izzard's customised shopping trolley. She asked him if they were rats, he replied yes, and they got to talking about rats for some considerable time. Joan Pearce's interest in fancy rats had stemmed from

A Himalayan kitten. It has yet to develop the full potential of its dark nose points.

attending an open university course in psychology, attending Sussex University the previous summer. Part of the course involved the use of rats in experiments concerning behaviour and rewards. It was love at first sight—Joan was smitten with rats and wanted one of her own as a pet. The next few months had been spent visiting various pet shops in the hope of getting a rat—all in vain. Several pet shop owners thought she was mad; "rats aren't pets, they're vermin!" being a typical response. Her last hope had been to attend the London Championship Show and perhaps find some "ratty people" there who could help her in her quest. She had somehow missed Geoff Izzard's exhibits, but here she was, at a bus stop outside the show hall (London's historical Alexandra Palace, no less), and she had met up with another rat lover. They both exchanged addresses, then later exchanged rats. Eventually, Eric Jukes and others pursuaded them both to join the L&SCMC and start exhibiting their rats. Publicity about the new rat fanciers in *Fur & Feather* brought a number of interested potential rat fanciers to light. As a result of this, support for the rat section at shows grew rapidly throughout the remainder of 1974 and 1975. In fact, so many rats began to be shown that several amendments and additions to the initially small rat show schedule of classes were made.

Eventually, thanks to more cajoling and advice from notable mouse fanciers, the rat fanciers decided to form a club or society purely for the exhibition of fancy rats. Thus it was that the inaugural meeting was held on January 13, 1976, and the *National Fancy Rat Society* was founded. Joan Pearce was the first Hon. Secretary/Treasurer, Geoff Izzard was Show Secretary/ Publicity Officer, Jon Strutt was Chairman, and Eric Smith was President. Professional geneticist Roy Robinson was appointed as Genetical Advisor to the society to advise on the development (or rediscovery) of different varieties of rat. By coincidence, at this time, Roy Robinson had developed a completely new variety of

Joining the rat fancy will not require much expense on your part—even if you start out with a show-quality animal.

rat: the curly-coated Rex. The fledgling society staged its first exhibition, just over a week after its formation, at the 1976 Bradford Championship Show, one of the most prestigious small livestock championship shows in the U.K. A fine display of fancy rats was staged, with the new Rex rats centre stage. A great deal of interest was shown in the rats by other fanciers and visitors to the show, and, as a result, a few new members were duly signed up. The very first N.F.R.S. Show was staged at Clymping, West Sussex, in conjunction with the Southern Hamster Club. A grand total of twenty-five rats were shown, equalling eighty-one entries, judged by Eric Smith. Best In Show went to an Argente adult (later renamed Silver Fawn), owned by Geoff Izzard—a very appropriate win. From that point on, the society progressed, with a growing membership, staging several shows in conjunction with other fancies and groups. Several members of the N.F.R.S. were still members of the L&SCMC, so the rat section at these shows still attracted high entries. The great milestone came on April 15, 1978, when the society staged a show entirely on its own in Surbiton Surrey. This was the very first genuine "rats only" show *ever*. Obviously, all the achievements of the N.F.R.S. over the years are too numerous to mention in great detail. However, notable points have been the establishment of contact and affiliation with other rat fancies and groups around the globe, which have sprung up since around 1978. Also, the N.F.R.S. publishes a bi-monthly journal, *Pro-Rat-A*, which covers a vast range of rat-related topics in every issue, for all grades of members, from the average pet rat keeper to the serious fancier. A comprehensive judges' training program has been developed over the years, ensuring that any new rat judges are trained to the highest quality in dealing with the task of judging all the varieties of fancy rat that abound today. The varieties, of course, have developed greatly over the years. When the N.F.R.S. was formed, the only varieties then available were Albino, Silver Fawn, Black Berkshire, Agouti and Hooded. That initial total of five now numbers over twenty-five,

Profile study of an Agouti rat. Presently, there are over twenty-five varieties of fancy rat.

with all the missing varieties from the days of the N.M.R.C. now rediscovered, with a number of completely new varieties having been developed. However, thus far, all varieties of fancy rat have been confined to *Rattus norvegicus*. Perhaps one day fancy specimens of *Rattus rattus* will make a return to the show bench?

One thing that has often puzzled me is that the rat fancy has succeeded since 1976, far beyond its previous influence, even spreading overseas. It is fast becoming an international fancy. The puzzling aspect of this is that all previous revivals or attempts to revive the fancy had failed, or fizzled out. Why did the original rat fancy die out?

My own personal opinion is that the *time* has to be right. The last quarter of the twentieth century has been particularly notable for the vast number of changes in everybody's daily life—worldwide. Therefore, as a result, people's perception of things can change rapidly. Possibly, whereas "rats" would have produced extreme revulsion many years ago, even when mentioned as pets, nowadays, people may be more inclined to accept the concept of rats as pets, as indeed they accept the concept of many hitherto unheard of or taboo subjects. Certainly, over the past fifteen years, I have personally witnessed the number of derogatory comments made about rats by other kinds of fanciers at shows diminish almost to the point of non-existence. More rats are sold as pets than ever before. Of course, the initial stigma of the word "rat" and its unsavoury associations are still there, but pet rats are accepted much more readily now than ever before. Perhaps, quite simply, the world

The Topaz (formerly Argente). This variety has a long, distinguished history on both sides of the Atlantic—and the North Sea.

A Pearl rat. As the rat fancy has grown, the negative image of the rat has diminished.

wasn't ready for fancy rats before 1976?

RAT SOCIETIES AROUND THE WORLD

Since the formation of the N.F.R.S. in 1976, the modern rat fancy has spread around the world. There are a number of groups in the United States of America, Sweden, Finland and Holland, plus a thriving German section of the N.F.R.S. Most groups, such as the N.F.R.S., do have an international membership, and several of these groups and societies are affiliated with each other, freely exchanging information and knowledge. Sometimes judges will officiate at shows staged in other countries by other groups, although, at present, this practice is fairly limited. Most of the varieties of fancy rat found in different countries are the same as originally bred in the U.K., with a few variations on the theme. Similarly, the Standards of Excellence to which fancy rats are judged by the various societies are based on the original British standards, which are, by and large, *genetically* accurate.

IS IT WORTH JOINING THE FANCY?

The answer in this case is a resounding "Yes." Even if you keep only one or two rats purely as pets, membership in a rat society and, by association, the rat fancy, can be very helpful. All the rat societies publish newsletters or journals, which are written *by* the members *for* the members. In this way, you can read up on all sorts of information about fancy rats. Apart from things like show reports and club business, which will always appear in such publications, you will find information about feeding, housing, daily care and the behaviour of fancy rats. You can share other rat lovers' experiences of keeping these delightful pets. Through the fancy you can make scores of new friends with a common, binding interest—the love of fancy rats. Often, you will find that such people share more than just one interest, which is a great bonus. I speak from personal experience, remember—I met my wife through the rat fancy, and we found that we had a great deal more in common besides rats. Obviously, I'm not going to guarantee that "you'll find your one true love or your money back on this book," but there are more benefits in joining a club or society devoted to fancy rats than not joining one. After all, there are more pet rat keepers nowadays, since the formation of the new rat fancy, than there ever were before!

ARE RATS FOR YOU?

So, if you are still a "ratless reader," now is the time to examine the requirements of actually *keeping* fancy rats. We will examine all aspects of the care of fancy rats, from their

Checking stock at a rat show. Attending such events offers the opportunity to meet new people who share the same interests as you.

selection, through housing, feeding, and health. After that, if you wish to take things a bit further, we shall examine the different varieties of fancy rat, how to exhibit them at shows, then onto breeding and genetics.

If, after all that lot, you're *still* not convinced, then you never will be, so I suggest you take up something else as a hobby, because if rats aren't for you, then you're reading the wrong book! "Nuff said!"

A Rat of Your Own

"The well seemed full of the creatures—all white, with eyes like rubies. He tried to count them—there must be a dozen at least."

Fame Is The Spur
by Howard
Spring, 1940

WHY A RAT?

I don't really like comparing animals to each other, especially pets. In fact, to some "animal folk," discussing the rival merits of different pets— sometimes even different breeds of the same animal—is tantamount to discussing politics and religion in one explosive package! However, *without* wishing to denigrate other pets and fancy livestock, I will strive to make some comparisons, all done from the point of view of practicality. Fancy rats are easy to keep. You can keep several rats together in one cage, unlike Syrian hamsters. They aren't as noisy as cavies, and you don't need to clean their cages out as often as is necessary with rabbits. All rats, and fancy rats in particular, are very clean animals and have very little natural odour. In fact, they don't smell at all as long as you keep their cages clean. They don't shed fur all over the place like a cat or a dog and you don't need to take them for walks (although some people do). They are easier to handle than lively gerbils, less delicate (and expensive!) than chinchillas, and more attentive than a goldfish. In fact, rats are altogether more affectionate, intelligent, playful and downright inventive than many other small animals. They are easy to feed, cheap to care for, and very stimulating companions. (It is a well-proven fact that

A happy rat owner and her pet. Rats can be fine companion animals.
They are active and playful and will delight you for hours on end.

people who keep pets—especially interesting and lively pets—live longer on average than people who have no pets at all). Fancy rats are easy to breed and may be bred in several attractive varieties. Their one major fault is that they usually don't live much longer than 2½ to 3 years.

WHO CAN OWN A FANCY RAT?

Anyone who wants a nice pet or good show animal can keep rats, as long as he applies the usual common-sense rules and care when keeping animals. A tame rat will never bite and can be handled safely even by young children. A fancy rat is a perfect pet for people of all ages. It fills a niche for anybody who wants a more intelligent and affectionate pet than a hamster or cavy but can't keep a cat or dog.

DECIDING TO OBTAIN A RAT

When you have made your decision to obtain a rat, there are a few questions that you must ask yourself:

- Why do you want a rat? Do you want it just as a pet, or also as a show animal that you can exhibit and breed?
- Do you want one or two rats, or more?
- What sex do you want your rat or rats to be?
- What variety of rat do you

Rats have a very quick growth rate, as you can see from the comparison below. The tiny rat is two days old; the fully furred rat is two weeks old.

In making your selection, you should first decide whether you want a pet-quality rat or a show-quality rat.

want to keep?

- Do you have the necessary space to house a rat or rats?
- If the rat is for a child, can you be sure that (a) the child wants a pet rat and (b) he will continue to care for it or will the novelty wear off?

Having considered all these points carefully, if you still want a pet-quality or show-quality fancy rat, next comes the business of selecting one.

SELECTION

Many people have told me over the years that they

didn't select their rat—*it* selected *them*. As rats are so intelligent and possess a high degree of empathy, I can well believe this, especially as it has happened to me. The rat I *wanted* may have been the ideal show specimen, but the rat I ended up *choosing*—or being chosen by—was not what could be considered a show specimen but was a really friendly, charming animal.

Pet shops stock a variety of fancy rats from which you can choose. If your pet shop doesn't carry the particular colour variety of fancy rat that you are looking for, perhaps the proprietor can special-order it for you. If not, you can try to contact a specialist breeder.

Naturally, you will want to make your selection from rats that are well maintained. When you visit the breeder, take careful note of the rats' environment. Do the animals have enough room to freely move about? Are

their cages clean? If not, then make your selection elsewhere.

The breeder will probably show you a number of young rats, called kittens, from which you will want to select your pet. First watch the breeder. If he or she is unduly cautious about picking up the kittens, then the chances are the animals aren't very tame. Here I must stress the point that, whereas all fancy rats are born "tame," that is, not wild, they still have to learn to accept humans and feel safe and confident in our presence. So don't expect incredibly docile kittens from the word go. Next, look at the rats. Are they alert and interested in their surroundings? Are they skittish and darting? Are they torpid and uninterested in their surroundings? An uninterested rat is as bad as a skittish one, so try for the happy medium. If the young rats are still with their mother, carefully

Rats can *sometimes* get along with other animals for short periods of time. Blondie, the Persian cat, and Fluke, the rat, have known each other for a long time and are quite comfortable in each other's presence.

observe her behaviour. If she is shy or aggressive, don't buy the kittens. Temperament is inherited, and you can be pretty certain that your rat will take after its mother. Temperament counts for a lot, and any good breeder will not breed a rat with a bad temper, no matter how good looking the animal is. However, don't be fooled into thinking that *all* show rats have bad temperament because they are ostensibly bred with a particular variety in mind. Nor does it follow that *all* mis-marked, so-called "pet-quality," rats have excellent temperament simply because they aren't bred for colour or markings. The breeder will no doubt let you handle some kittens. Now you must check that the rat is in good health. Gently pick up the rat by placing your hand over its back and lifting it onto the palm of your other hand. If the kitten is a little nervous, gently grip the base of the tail to pacify it. (Small rats may be quickly lifted from one place to another by holding the base of the tail. However, you must *never* hold a rat by the tip of the tail, especially an adult rat, as the tail may "skin" or even break). Now that you are holding the kitten, feel its bone structure. A healthy rat should be neither too scrawny, with arched back, nor too fat, although kittens often have puppy fat (unintentional pun), so make allowances for this. The coat should be in good condition, bright and sleek, not dull and lacklustre. However, the fur of a kitten is somewhat softer than that of an adult rat, and several varieties are much paler as kittens. Kittens of the curly-coated Rex variety often sport bald patches in their fur, which is acceptable, as they moult several times before their coats develop fully. However, a smooth-coated rat should have no bald or bare patches at all. Checking the rest of the rat, make sure that the eyes are clear and bright, the nose clean and free from discharge. If the rat is constantly sneezing or wheezing, don't buy it! The ears should be erect, clean and whole. Check the tail and genitals for cleanliness; any excessive staining is a sign of diarrhoea. Reputable breeders will not sell a kitten younger than six weeks of age. In fact, if rats are being offered for sale at a show, then there are strict rules on the age of sale stock: nothing younger than six weeks may be sold. Very young kittens, or kittens from a big litter, although eating solid food, may still be suckling from their mother, so be sure to check on this very important point. Finally, if the kitten you are buying is a doe (female) and is aged over eight weeks, be sure to check that it has been separated from its brothers, as rats can be sexually mature at this age and the last thing you want is a young, pregnant doe!

HOW MANY RATS?

The question of how many rats you wish to keep is extremely important. Bear in mind that, unlike hamsters for instance, rats are gregarious animals. That is, they enjoy the company of their own kind. It is perfectly acceptable to have a single rat as a pet, but in that case you need to spend a lot of time with it, in order to return its affections and stimulate it mentally. A lonely rat can be a very unhappy rat! If you really want a happy and contented pet rat, then get *two* rats. Obviously, if you don't want to breed them, then make

A healthy rat will be bright eyed and alert.

sure they are the same sex. Ideally, a single-sex pair should be of the same age, litter mates being ideal. Two rats can become as tame as one if you spend enough time with them. Whilst you are busy elsewhere, the rats are company for each other. Being inventive and playful animals, especially when they are kittens, they can get up to all sorts of fun and games together.

BUCK OR DOE?

Whether you are keeping one rat or a single-sex pair, you will probably wonder what sex is best in a rat. Whether you choose bucks (males) or does (females) is purely a matter of personal choice, as both sexes make equally good pets. A few points worth considering in your choice:

- Bucks are bigger than does. (The average adult buck weighs in at around 500 to 600 grams, a doe at 200–300 grams.) Bucks are not as lively as does. In fact, some could be considered to be downright lazy, although this varies from rat to rat. Does are quite active and lively. If you want a big cuddly rat who will sit on your lap, then choose a

buck. If you want a really playful rat, choose a doe.
- One thing that often makes people choose a doe as opposed to a buck is the fact that bucks often "mark their territory" by leaving small traces of urine wherever they go. Does—unless one happens to be a very dominant individual—seldom do this.
- On average, does live slightly longer than bucks. Statistically, the average lifespan of an adult buck rat is between 2 and 2¼ years. The average lifespan of a doe can be anything up to 2½ years. Obviously, there are exceptions either way, just as some people "go on" for ever.

The foregoing statements are, of course, generalisations. I'm sure that there are plenty of rat owners out there who are on the point of reaching for a note pad to write me an indignant letter contradicting my remarks.

Please don't—I really hate generalisations and statistics. For example, how can the average British family consist of 2 adults, 2.5 children and 1.5 dogs?! Animals never comply to a rigid set of rules... probably because they never read the books written about them!

Obviously, if you wish to breed fancy rats, then you may well want a pair or trio of mixed sexes.

At first, go gently with your new pet, and allow it to become used to you.

A freshly bathed rat. Rats of light colouration may require a bit more grooming than those with dark coloured fur.

WHAT VARIETY?

Obviously, which variety you choose to keep reflects your taste in colours and patterns. Some people get hyped up over Hoodeds, whilst others swoon over Silver Fawns. It really is a matter of personal choice and, if you are contemplating breeding and exhibiting, then you need to carefully consider how difficult a particular variety may be to perfect, irrespective of like or dislike.

Some varieties have different temperaments, or, to be more specific, different bloodlines of different varieties vary in temperament. All fancy rats are *tame*, as I have stated previously, but some are more placid or excitable than others. I'm not going to stick my neck out here and say which varieties are best in this respect, as this would only be my personal opinion and could cause offence to fanciers of particular varieties. Suffice it to say, you, the potential rat owner, should check every aspect of your potential pet carefully.

Housing

When I first started keeping fancy rats it was virtually impossible to find a suitable cage. Today, fortunately, this is not the case. Like all other animals, rats need housing in an environment that suits their needs in all respects. One good rule of thumb is that a cage can often be too small, but seldom too large. Rats often stand on their hind legs, usually to reach or sniff at something. This is a perfectly natural stance for them, so whatever cage they are housed in should be tall enough for them to stand upright in. They are also very active and inventive animals, and enjoy climbing, which is good exercise for their muscles and actually stimulates growth in young kittens. If the cage denies them this factor, then it is unsuitable. I'd never have anything to do with laboratory cages. They may

A simple plastic container can make an ideal bedroom for your rats.

be designed to house rats walking on all fours, but they do not permit them to stand upright or climb very easily. A cage should, of course, also have sufficient width and length to allow free movement and a good area of free floor space. The minimum-size cage for a pair of rats should be 24" x 12" x 12" (60 x 30 x 30 cms). An ideal manufactured cage should have a base of metal or hard plastic, with wire mesh or bars making up the main body of the cage. The gauge of the wire or bars should not be such so as to allow the rat to squeeze through. A gauge of ½" (125 mm) is quite sufficient. Do *not* contemplate using a cage that does not have a solid floor base. Cages with mesh floors are highly unsuitable for rats' feet and can lead to accidents. Also, sawdust or wood shavings must cover the floor area, which is not possible with an open-mesh floor. If you have no choice but to purchase a wire-mesh-floor cage, you must ensure that the bedding is piled deep enough to more than adequately cover the

floor. Cages with frontage that is a combination of bars and glass are acceptable, but do check carefully how much glass is included. Condensation can build up easily and cause problems, especially if the cage is placed in a very warm environment.

Of course, it is possible to utilise other types of animal cages to house your rats. Large bird cages are ideal, having good dimensions—plenty of height—and strong metal bars. Aviaries can be simply adapted to the needs of rats. My wife and I constructed two excellent cages out of pre-prepared aviary panels. The finished "ratvaries" stand 6' tall (180cms), with a width and length of 3' (90 cms). They are spacious enough to house up to 15 rats (of one sex!) comfortably.

By far, one of the best "alternative" rat cages is an aquarium tank. These may be purchased at a reasonable price (depending on size and construction)

Rats like branches on which they can climb, so always include them if your cage is large enough.

This is an ideal homemade cage, designed by Rachel Rodham of the National Fancy Rat Society, England. If desired, the cage can be sectioned off into individual units.

from any good pet shop.

Most pet stores sell or can order wire screen covers that will fit aquariums of all sizes.

If you are handy, have the tools, and don't mind spending extra time, you can make your own tank cover. Some form of weight will probably be needed to hold the lid in place and keep your rats in, but this does not present too great a problem.

Having obtained your rat's housing, you must now turn your attention to furnishing it. The floor area needs a covering. I have seen some people use newspaper, which is *not* advisable. The rats rip it up for one thing; the other is that printer's ink can be poisonous if consumed. So, for the *substrate*, as floor covering is trendily known nowadays, use either sawdust or wood shavings. These should be bought from a pet shop or supplier, ideally, as these will probably have been pre-treated with disinfectant to kill any lurking germs that could harm your rat. Sawdust or shavings gathered direct from a sawmill or timber yard are obviously not pre-treated and can contain several impurities. It is best to play it safe—after all, sawdust and shavings are not terribly expensive. Some fanciers use peat or even cat litter of various sorts as substrate, but personally I don't rate this at all highly. For one thing, these compounds can make the rat very dirty! One final point about sawdust or shavings: always aim for the best possible quality. My motto is: "Not so fine as to go up the nose, nor so big as to scrape the toes." Aim for a happy medium wherever possible.

Bedding is largely a matter of personal choice. Some fanciers maintain that their rats simply don't need it or use it if it is provided. However, there is nothing wrong with providing bedding, especially if your rat is housed in a shed outdoors. There are lots of different brands of animal bedding to be found in the pet market: By far the best is shredded paper,

A typical shed rattery.

preferably packaged and pre-medicated. Again, avoid newsprint, as it may be poisonous. Fresh hay is always a good option, as it helps improve the rat's coat, acting as a sort of comb.

The rats will also eat some of it, as it provides good roughage to the diet. However, be careful where you obtain the hay. Badly prepared bags or bales can contain nettles (which may not be harmful to a rat but can be pretty nasty for you!), pieces of stone and the scourge of the rat fancier: mites.

My advice regarding cotton wool and man-made fibre bedding is, quite simply, forget it! The hard strands can easily become entangled 'round the rat's legs, feet and throat. I have seen some animals, especially young rat kittens, have their toes severed by this type of bedding!

EXERCISE AND TOYS

As previously mentioned, rats do like to climb. They are quite arboreal in their habits to the extent that they like resting and sleeping on a perch or platform raised off the floor of the cage. Thick bird-perches can be purchased from pet shops and easily fitted into most cages. Failing this, some branches will suffice, but make sure they are clean before putting them in the cage. The rats will also enjoy chewing these and exercising their teeth. Small platforms can be made out of a square or oblong piece of chipboard and fixed onto the bars of a cage. Similarly, swings can be hung from wires from the top of the cage, or the mesh lid of an aquarium. Ropes are also a firm favourite and may be hung from bars or mesh lids, allowing the rats to scurry up and down them with great agility. Metal bird ladders can also indulge a rat's love of climbing. Exercise wheels are not a good idea. For a start, most are too small for rats to use. Rats might also trap their tails in the spokes of the wheels and cause serious damage. In any event, all rats should be regularly allowed out of their cages for exercise.

A mother rat nursing her litter. If you plan to breed rats, you will have to make provision for additional housing.

Stimulation can be provided by an empty jar or a tin can with all sharp edges removed. Some rats like small balls to push around, such as a large marble or ball bearing. I don't use toy boots and the like made out of plastic. For one thing, any rat will probably chew them up, and several of these toys have small holes in them whereby rats could trap their heads.

Those large incisor teeth need exercise and honing,

so a piece of smooth wood for your rats to chew will be ideal. Cardboard tubes from the insides of paper towel and toilet tissue rolls are also useful in this way. These tubes will also provide a good deal of amusement for young rats, especially to run in and out of, like tunnels.

CAGE LOCATION

The location of your rat's cage is very important. Rats thrive best at a room temperature no more than 23°C (73°F). If kept indoors, your rat's cage must be situated on a shelf or another surface that is raised off the ground. It must not be placed in direct sunlight, which could prove fatal, especially if the rat is housed in an aquarium tank. Also, do not place the cage in direct draughts or a near powerful source of heat, such as a fireplace or radiator. Although they are hardy animals, rats may *not* be housed outside in the same way as rabbits and cavies, so don't even try. Of course, rats may be housed in a shed or outbuilding, as long as the ambient temperature is not too hot or too cold.

THE RATTERY

Many fanciers who keep large numbers of rats have what is known as a "rattery." This can either be a garden shed, garage or outbuilding, or even a room in the house. Whatever, the same basic principles apply.

Firstly, a shed or outbuilding should be a solid construction, measuring no less than 6' x 4' (1.80m x 1.20m). The roof should have a covering of roofing felt, which must obviously not let water in. The wood should be painted inside and out with a preservative, again to protect against damp, and this should be re-painted every two to three years. Also, the shed should ideally be raised a little off the ground, usually placed on bricks, thereby preventing seeping dampness. A floor covering such as lino provides added protection and is easy to sweep and clean.

Ventilation is obviously important, but there is no real need to go in for air conditioning systems unless you live in a very warm climate, in which case use the best possible. Windows can easily be opened on hot days, and a simple guard made out of wire mesh will prevent cats from sneaking in. Similarly, a simple screen door can be made for use when the main door is open.

Lighting is best provided by electricity, either wired in from the mains or hooked up in the form of an extension lead and light bulb socket run from the house when required. Oil and gas lamps can be decidedly dangerous, especially with sawdust, etc. in the area. Heating is not really necessary, as

Wire mesh is durable and can make a good top for your pet's cage.

plenty of good bedding will keep the rats warm. However, if you think it is necessary, a small electric heater is best—again, oil and gas are dangerous in a rattery. Ensure that a maximum temperature of

15°C (59°F) is maintained by a thermostat.

A plumbing system is rather unnecessary, not to mention costly. A hose can be run from an outside tap, of course, but when tending to their stock most fanciers tend to use buckets of water brought in from the house. However, the sky's the limit, so if you can afford the cost, there's absolutely nothing to stop you from having water and electricity run into your rattery for convenience.

If the rattery is a room within your house, just ensure that there is adequate lighting and ventilation. A suitable floor covering is a must. Lino is ideal for cleaning; a carpet is definitely a bad idea. Sawdust and hay are very difficult to sweep up! Failing an easy-to-clean covering, just leave bare floorboards. Furnishings for the rattery are simple, but essential. Strong shelving for your rats' cages should be placed along the walls, ideally bracketed into position, thus providing stability. Whether the shelving is metal, wood, or even plastic is immaterial, but do be careful that damp conditions do not warp wooden shelving, or turn metal shelving rusty! Keep all unused food bowls, medicines, equipment, etc., in cupboards. Dry food should be stored in a closed bin or air-tight container. You will also find that a table, bench or worksurface will be useful when you wish to inspect a particular rat. Always wipe the table clean with a damp cloth after use. A well-maintained rattery makes an ideal base to direct your operations within the fancy, and can even enhance your rats, showing them off in pleasant surroundings.

MAINTENANCE

Cages should be cleaned out once a week, with all sawdust and bedding replaced. Daily tidying up can be done by removing

Rats in their sleeping quarters. Do not leave any perishable food in the cage once your rat has eaten his meal.

Items needed to set up your rat's home: wood shavings, bedding material, food bowl, and gravity water bottle.

any perishable uneaten food and clearing any faeces from the toilet area. Some rats can be very helpful by maintaining a "toilet corner" in their cages. Corners tend to accumulate the worst of the week's mess, and a wallpaper scraper is ideal for removing such matter.

Alternatively, corner blocks may be made quite simply and glued into place, thus helping to keep the cage clean. Every three months or so, it is a good idea to thoroughly wash and disinfect the cage in order to eradicate any lingering dirt, which could lead to germs.

Feeding

One of the main reasons why, as a species, the rat has fared so successfully in the wild is its all-encompassing omnivorous diet. In fact, it is quite hard to define something that the rat will *not* eat, or try to eat.

Fancy rats, although omnivorous, are somewhat more discerning about what they eat. In order to reach a level of good health and show quality, a well

Fancy rats can be somewhat discriminating in what they choose to eat and will carefully sniff any food item that is offered to them.

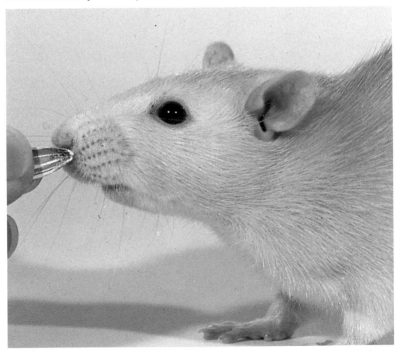

balanced diet must be received daily. Feeding is one of those areas akin to "politics and religion" amongst many fanciers: everybody has his own preferred feeding method. However, the basic core of every fancier's method is the same—to feed the rat well. Of course, it is often the case that some folk can spoil their rats and feed them *too* well and too often. An adult rat needs to be fed once a day, normally in the evening when it is generally most active. Alternatively, a half-sized meal in the morning, followed by a similar-sized meal in the evening, is acceptable.

The staple diet for the fancy rat should consist of dry food. Mixed corn, wheat, cereals, biscuits, flaked maize and dried, crushed peas are an ideal mixture. There are several proprietary brands of dry food available on the market, but not all are totally suitable for rats. Hamster mix, for instance,

Fresh fruits and vegetables can be offered to your rat, but consider them as supplements to the basic diet of dry food.

can sometimes contain too many sunflower seeds and peanuts. These items are fine as a treat, or in a very small quantity mixed into the main food, but they are very rich in protein and can cause skin problems if fed in excess. Many times I've had rat keepers contact me at their wits' end about their rats' being covered with spots and wondering what sort of mites have caused them because no treatment is working. The suggestion to change their pets' diet, which hitherto has contained lots of sunflower seeds and peanuts, works wonders. So be careful of overdoing the protein. Ideally, sunflower seeds and peanuts should be reserved purely as tidbits.

Mono-diets are not a good idea in my honest opinion. Laboratory pellets or rabbit pellets may well contain a balance of vitamins and proteins, but

Select food bowls that are sturdy and non-tippable. Your pet shop offers a wide variety of accessories for your pet.

An occasional treat is fine—just don't overdo it.

many rats, not surprisingly, get totally bored with them and sometimes even refuse to eat. Variety in the diet is all important. Other constituents of a healthy diet can include wholemeal bread, breakfast cereals (non-sugared brands), some types of dog chow and cooked potato, rice and occasionally some cooked meat in small quantities. There are some brands of puppy food, usually mixed with water, that promote rapid growth in youngsters. A little of this goes a long way, so don't fall into the mono-diet trap and feed your rats on this exclusively. Nutritional studies have shown evidence that *overfeeding* this type of food to dogs and smaller animals can lead to problems.

Supplements to the basic diet need to be given. Vegetables and fruit provide vitamins and additional moisture, together with folic acid, which helps red blood cells to mature in the animal. It is best to avoid vegetables such as onions, and citrus fruits, which are too acidic for small animals' stomachs to stand with regular feeding. Ideal fruits and vegetables are: apple, tomato, celery, carrots,

You can feed your pet its main meal once a day (preferably in the evening), or you can feed it two half-sized meals (one in the morning and one in the evening).

cabbage and lettuce. Fruits and vegetables should only be given every second or third day and purely as a supplement to the dry diet, not an alternative. Ensure that the quantities are balanced accordingly. Overfeeding of these foods can lead to diarrhoea.

In their wild state, rats are, to some degree, insectivorous. Mealworms provide a good source of protein and may be fed now and again as a treat—but not to excess. Table scraps can form a good part of the rat's supplementary diet. Usually, if you eat it, your rat will eat it. My rats do very nicely with such table scraps as potato, spaghetti, peas, sweetcorn, rice, pastry and pancakes. Always ensure that the food is cooked and doesn't contain salt, pepper, or strong, hot spices or sauces. Meat bones can be given now and again, as the rats enjoy gnawing the meat off them and then gnawing into the bones to extract the marrow.

Fresh water must be offered daily. It is also important to clean the water container on a regular basis.

Not only is it extra nutrition, but it helps to exercise their teeth. However, be careful to avoid "splintery" bones such as poultry and fish. Fish bones can also be small and very sharp and might get lodged in your rat's throat

A young rat kitten suckles his mother while his siblings sleep. Rat kittens can get a very strong grip on their mother's nipples.

and could cause death. If you feed cooked fish to your rat, always ensure that the fish has been boned beforehand.

Always put your rat's food in a strong earthenware bowl that cannot be easily tipped. It is true that rats like scratching around in their sawdust for tidbits, so putting a little dry food on the cage floor will give them something to do. However,

don't put too much down, as the sawdust will be made very dirty very quickly in this way. All perishable uneaten food must be removed within 24 hours.

Fresh drinking water must be given daily. It is best to provide this in a gravity water bottle. This may be fixed to the bars of the cage, or suspended on a hanger looped over the side of a tank or suspended from the lid of the tank. Be careful not to allow the spout of the bottle to touch the floor of the cage, as this will cause the gravity action, which will drain the bottle. The result: one wet cage. Water bowls are best avoided, as rats either kick sawdust into them, or defecate in them.

VITAMINS AND SUPPLEMENTS

Pet shops stock a variety of vitamin and mineral supplements for small rodents. It is true that if your rat's diet is well balanced, then it does not need to be "dosed up" with this or that supplement. However, the occasional addition of a supplement in the food or water should present no problems and can only do good, as long as you work the dosage out correctly!

Unlike cavies, monkeys and men, rats produce their own vitamin C, so they don't really need a great intake of this vitamin. Like rabbits, rats practice *refection*, that is, eating of their droppings for further absorption of minerals. Rats' droppings contain naturally-produced

A proper diet will help to keep your rat's coat in tiptop condition.

You owe it to your pet to keep him and his accommodations in good order, for his physical and mental well being. To do otherwise is nothing less than gross cruelty.

Vitamin K, produced by bacteria in the gut.

Preparations such as wheat germ and cod liver oil can easily be added to dry food. Alternatively, cod liver oil capsules are available, and rats do relish these, generally. One capsule per rat per week is quite sufficient. However, a little extra a week or so before a show can enhance coat condition very nicely.

TREATS

Most people enjoy eating the foods that are bad for them—and rats share this trait. They particularly like sweet things, such as chocolate drops. One or two chocolate drops a week is fine, but don't overdo such treats, as they can cause obesity and tooth decay if fed in excessive quantities.

Of course, treats and tidbits are quite useful if you are taming your rat, or even training it to perform some sort of trick. Always keep the treats small and to a minimum. Better still, try rewarding the rat with something healthy, like a dried raisin or a piece of cheese.

Ailments

Like most aspects of keeping any animal, the health of your rat is largely a matter of common sense on your part. Keeping the rat at an even temperature, well housed, well fed, given plenty of exercise—all these are the cornerstones of maintaining your rat's health.

Having said that, however, there might be times when your rat will be

This rat is nearly three years old. Extra special, gentle care must be taken when handling elderly and very young rats.

ill. In the case of problems such as bites or spots, the animal's condition is quite obvious. Other health problems are not so easily recognised. A general guide to determine whether or not your rat is feeling poorly is its general appearance and behaviour. If your rat is hunched over, with a staring (fluffed up) coat, dull eyed and generally listless, then you can be fairly sure that something is amiss and then start to check for more complex signs of ill health.

If ever you are in any doubt about your rat's health, by far the best course of action is to *take it to your vet*! A few years back, vets were not very well versed on the ailments of fancy rats, but this situation is, thankfully, changing rapidly, with much better reference material on rat health available to vets. However, in the same way that most people don't run to their doctor every time they

sneeze, so it is not always necessary to rush your rat to the vet with certain ailments. There may also be times when it is not possible to get to the vet's, in which case you will need to know how to treat different ailments and conditions.

The following list of ailments and treatments is not, by any means, a complete veterinary guide to rat health. *Don't* try to treat an unknown condition yourself. It all comes down to common sense and knowing when is the right time to attempt treatment yourself or refer the ailing rat to a vet.

WOUNDS AND ABSCESSES

Wounds are generally caused by rats fighting with each other—especially adult bucks. It isn't often that fights get out of hand, but occasionally one rat may sustain a nasty wound that may well develop into an abscess.

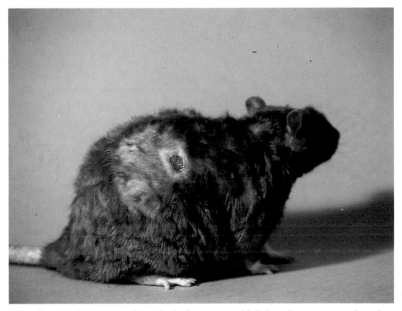

This Rex rat has a semi-healed abscess, which has been opened and drained. A scab is now forming.

First, check how the wound was caused. Was it through some sharp object in the rat's cage or was it due to a fight? If you suspect the latter and feel that the rats have not resolved their differences, split them up. Next, check the extent of the wound. If the wound is very deep, so that the skin has split and muscle tissue is visible, or worse, damaged, then this will need suturing by a vet within six hours, or the skin will "begin to die." A shallow wound should be bathed with warm water, then apply iodine. The wound may need bathing for a couple of days, but if adequately cleaned up, a scab should develop and new skin will form naturally.

If an abscess does develop, this will need draining regularly. A piece of tissue paper will suffice. Gently squeeze the pus out of the abscess and bathe the area with warm water. A good measure is to apply a couple of drops of hydrogen peroxide to the open cavity.

The hydrogen peroxide will start to bubble on contact with the infected tissue and will force the remaining pus out of the cavity. Continue to "drain and flush" daily, until all the pus is gone and a scab forms over new flesh.

BROKEN LEGS

Very rarely, a rat may break a leg whilst climbing. Unless the damaged limb is giving the rat a lot of

Rats are very clean animals and will spend a great deal of time meticulously grooming themselves.

A rat with a large, but benign, tumor.

distress, you do not need to do anything to it... especially as splinting a rat's leg is extremely difficult. Just ensure that the rat is kept in a quiet environment and don't let it climb too much or run around. The leg bone should soon heal and, although the leg may not look perfectly straight, it will be acceptable for the rat's use.

A very badly damaged leg could be amputated by a vet, but account should be taken of how this will affect the rat's life. A rat can manage on three legs, but quality of life must be your prime consideration in such a case.

COLDS

Rats catch colds very easily. A sudden drop in temperature or a draughty room may cause this very quickly. If you are transporting your rat to and from shows during the winter, be sure that you don't let it get too cold or inhale icy air, which can prove fatal. The symptoms of a cold in a rat is staring coat, general hunched appearance and discharge from the eyes and nose. Usually, any discharge is red, which can be alarming as it looks like blood, but it is merely the colouration of the discharged mucus. The rat will also begin sneezing and wheezing.

The first thing to do is to isolate the sick rat from any cage mates. Place it in a smaller cage and keep it warm. A higher temperature in this case is acceptable. A good source of extra heat is to place a lamp over the cage. Give the rat plenty to drink and keep it quiet. Extra food in the form of a warm mash may also be provided and help the rat build up its strength. It is important to treat a cold quickly, as this may lead to pneumonia, which is much more difficult to treat successfully. In this case, the rat's breathing will become progressively heavier, coupled with a rapid weight loss. In this instance, prompt veterinary treatment is required, and the vet may attempt an injection of penicillin. Sadly, however, pneumonia is very difficult to treat, so always ensure that an ailment as simple as a cold is quickly treated—before it leads to pneumonia!

EAR INFECTIONS

Ear infections are typified by the rat holding its head to one side and, in bad cases, falling over. This may be due to a viral infection in the inner ear, affecting the delicate balance organs. Thus far, there is no rock-solid treatment, although an antimicrobial agent, best administered by a vet, does usually give some relief. Recovery, however, is usually only partial, and the rat may still have its balance affected in different degrees for the rest of its life. Being a viral infection, this is not inherited, so afflicted rats can still be used for breeding.

Other infections may be bacterial, which cause severe inflammation of the ear drum. The ear drum will

Always wash your hands after handling a rat that is ill.

eventually burst and infection will be discharged. Apply an antimicrobial agent and bathe any discharge away. The rat will generally soon recover.

EYE INFECTIONS

Eye infections can be caused by a number of different factors. Dust in the eye, draughts, a scratch, or even a secondary infection following a cold can cause such infections. Usually, a clear discharge will be seen around the eyes. This is treated by

The more you know about your pet's regular behavior, the easier it will be for you to determine when he is not feeling well.

bathing the eyes with very slightly salty warm water. Your vet will generally prescribe an antimicrobial agent or an antibiotic ointment to fully clear up the infection.

Older rats may suffer from cataracts, which is a greying of the eye lens, giving the eye a grey/white appearance. This impairs the rat's vision. Cataracts cannot be treated and, as they generally occur in old rats, any benefits would not be long term. If the rat is still actively engaged in breeding, *don't* breed from it, as cataracts are inherited.

DIARRHOEA

Also known as scours. In the normal way of things, a healthy rat's droppings should be solid and dry, dark brown in colour. If they are found to be very loose and pale, even runny, then this could mean the beginning of diarrhoea.

There are many causes for scouring. Most commonly, it is caused by feeding the rat too much green food. The simple cure in this case is to change the diet to dry food only for a few days. After this, you can try gradually increasing the rat's intake of green food again. If loose droppings or diarrhoea reoccur, don't feed the rat any food for a couple of days; just give it rice water—that is, water in which rice has been boiled

All fruit and vegetables that you offer to your rat should be fresh. If they are not, digestive problems could result.

(*without* salt!). Liquid charcoal is equally useful in stabilising the rat's gut. After this, feed the rat white bread and milk, then gradually replace this with its usual diet. Stress can also be a factor in causing scouring. Sometimes rats, especially kittens, become very stressed when travelling to shows, which causes them to scour badly. Usually, this corrects itself when the rat returns to its familiar surroundings and/or gets used to travelling.

Diarrhoea can also be caused by infections in the rat's gut. A course of antibiotics from the vet, together with a dry-food diet, will generally correct most infections.

CONSTIPATION

This condition is the opposite of diarrhoea, but every bit as distressing and harmful to the rat. In simple terms, the rat is unable to defecate. The symptoms are obvious, as the rat has a swollen stomach, sits hunched back and refuses to eat. Again, there are various causes: sometimes some form of infection, occasionally stress related, but mostly caused by an imbalance in the diet—usually too much dry food and not enough greenfood or fibre.

If the rat will eat it, try giving it lots of lettuce, which will act as an emetic. If the rat will not eat, try giving it some corn oil, via a pipette (or eyedropper). When the rat has recovered, continue to feed the greenfood as part of the balanced diet, but be careful not to feed too much, or this can quickly lead to diarrhoea.

DEHYDRATION

This is often a side effect of an illness. Rats get badly dehydrated whilst suffering from diarrhoea, due to the sudden loss in bodily fluids. The symptoms are rapid weight loss, staring coat and hunched

A rat that is in good health will react very quickly to any stimulus in its environment.

appearance. To check for dehydration, gently pinch the rat's scruff. If the skin lacks elasticity and will not revert to its normal shape, then the rat is definitely dehydrated. Give it plenty of water. Generally, a dehydrated rat will take no interest in food or water, so you may have to carefully force some water mixed with glucose into its mouth, via a pipette. When feeding a rat this way, be careful not to force the water in too hard or fast, as this may run back through the rat's nostrils and choke it! Keep the rat warm, as dehydration lowers body temperature. Once the rat gets some fluids back into its system, it should perk up considerably.

MITES

These minute parasites can cause a lot of problems in a rattery if untreated. There are many different species of mite, which can be introduced to rats in a variety of ways, most often via infested hay. Also, take extra care if ever you are introducing rats from another stud into your own stud. You never can tell where infestations lie. The symptoms of a mite infection are quite obvious bald patches in the rat's fur, and spots and scabs on the skin. Treatment is simple, but must be carried out quickly. All infected rats should be dipped in an anti-mite solution. This kind of preparation can be bought from most vets or is available on prescription. The preparation, usually in powdered form, is added to a bowl of warm water. You must then dip the rat in this solution as directed by the vet, but take care not to let any of the solution get into the rat's eyes or ears.

The rat should then be dried as much as possible with a towel. Sufficient residue of the solution will remain in the rat's fur and will be effective to kill the mites. The preparation is not toxic to the rat in small quantities, so when the rat washes itself it should suffer no ill effects, provided that you have followed the instructions carefully and mixed the "dip" correctly.

Prevention is better than cure, of course. One effective way to kill off any possible mite infestations is to use patent fly killers, which can be hung in the rattery or in the vicinity of your rat's cage. (It should be noted that some rats have become ill from these devices' having been placed too close to their cages, so be alert to any changes in your rat's behaviour when they are in use.)

Serious mite infections, such as demodectic mange, require veterinary treatment, as regular

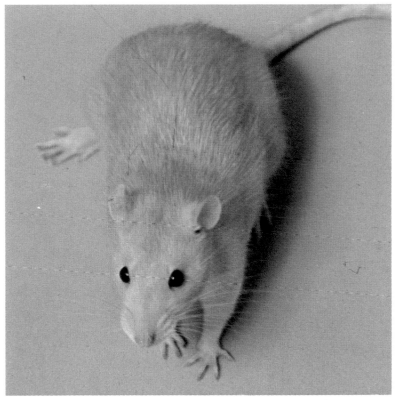

Check your pet's coat regularly for mites or any other kind of parasitic invasion.

methods will not always prove effective if such an infection is too far gone on an infected rat.

SPOTS AND SORES

If a rat develops spots or sores on its skin, usually under the chin, its owner

A gravity water bottle is the best way to provide your pet with water as it prevents the soiling of the water supply with droppings and cage-lining material.

often thinks that they are caused by mites. If referred to a vet, this diagnosis is, again more often than not, borne out and the rat is treated as for mites, by dipping in an anti-mite solution. However, it often happens that the spots and sores do *not* disappear, and the rat continues to scratch itself and appears uncomfortable. In this kind of instance, the spots and sores are *not* mite related, but are, in fact, caused by a dietary allergy or reaction.

Treatment is simple. First of all, check carefully what you are feeding the rat. If there are a lot of sunflower seeds or peanuts in its diet, then this indicates an excess of protein. Some prepared dryfood mixtures also contain lots of extra protein, as does too much meat in any form. The build-up of excess protein in the body causes skin inflammation, which is made worse by the rat scratching to quell the irritation. Next, remove all the offending food and feed the rat purely on rice, bread and some vegetables for a few days. Try adding some vitamin B to the rat's drinking water to counteract the proteins in its system. The spots and sores can be treated with a simple antiseptic ointment,

The eyes, ears, and nose should be clean and free of any signs of discharge.

preferably prescribed for animal use. After a few days, the skin complaint will clear up, and you can gradually start feeding the rat its usual diet again, but obviously being careful not to include too many protein-rich items. Once the rat has suffered this sort of skin

Rats are subject to heatstroke so keep room temperatures at a moderate level. If you have a shed-type rattery, ensure that it is properly ventilated.

complaint, it often recurs at the first hint of too much protein in the diet, so care must be taken with the rat's diet in the future.

HEATSTROKE

As previously stated, it is essential to keep the rat at an even temperature as much as possible. If room temperature exceeds 25°C (80°F), the rat may suffer heatstroke. The symptoms are alarmingly obvious, with the rat lying down, panting, with its eyes wide and staring. It will then fall into

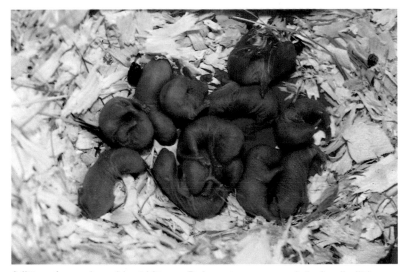

A litter of one-day-old rat kittens. Baby rats are especially fragile little creatures and, like elderly rats, are subject to hypothermia.

a comatose state and, if not treated immediately, will surely die. Remove the rat to a cool, shady area and sponge it down carefully with cold water in order to lower its body temperature. As soon as the rat shows signs of consciousness, make it drink some water, preferably with a slight dash of salt. Keep the rat quiet and cool, with plenty of liquids and vegetables within easy reach. Sadly, rats often die of kidney failure or heart attacks brought on by heatstroke, so prevention, as always, is better than cure. Keep room temperatures stable!

HYPOTHERMIA

Just as damaging as excessively high temperatures, excessively cold temperatures can also prove fatal to rats. Although rats can withstand cold better than heat, they cannot endure extreme cold for long. The rat will become lethargic, with a staring coat. Its body will be cold to the touch. Place the rat in a box well packed with bedding in a very warm area—perhaps in front of a radiator or fire. Try to make the rat drink a tiny bit of brandy to liven it up, then follow this with warm sugar water.

Very young or very elderly rats are very prone to hypothermia, so take extra care with them.

RESPIRATORY INFECTIONS

Fanciers often talk in shocked, hushed tones about the dreaded "snuffles," which can wipe out whole studs of livestock. The simple fact is, there are many different types of respiratory infection in rats, caused by a variety of reasons and all varying in severity. Few prove fatal, however.

The first signs of a respiratory problem are that the rat sneezes a lot, discharging clear fluid from its nose. In many cases, it may not be an illness at all, but a reaction to very fine sawdust, in which case change the sawdust for a substrate that is not so fine, such as wood shavings. If the sneezing continues, the chances are that it is a viral infection, in which case you should consult the vet. Rats with respiratory problems can still breed normally (the diseases are not congenital), but the rats may not be shown, as they can pass infection on to other fanciers' stock.

Genuine "snuffles" are bacterial and cause the rat to wheeze and "rattle," as it develops a sinus/chest infection. Again, treatment may include the administration of antibiotics. Untreated snuffles could lead to pneumonia, so always treat suspected infections quickly. Any rats suffering

When allowing your rat to run around for exercise, be careful that it doesn't chew any electrical wiring.

in this way should be isolated from other rats in the stud to prevent infection.

OVERGROWN TEETH

Being rodents, gnawing is a natural action for rats. Generally, a well-kept rat will have plenty of opportunity to exercise its incisor teeth by chewing on a specially provided block of wood or a branch. Hard food in the diet also acts in honing down teeth. Occasionally, however, when such gnawing aids are absent, a rat's teeth may easily become overgrown. The other common factor in causing overgrown teeth is a condition known as *malocclusion*, which is a deformity of the teeth or jaw, being either congenital (i.e., in a particular bloodline/strain) or by injury. The upper and lower incisors no longer meet and continue to grow, often ending up penetrating the jaw itself, or the rat's cheeks. Usually, malocclusion, if congenital, will manifest itself in young kittens. Whatever the cause, the first indication of overgrown or deformed teeth is that the rat suddenly loses weight, as it is unable to eat properly, so food will also remain uneaten. The jaw and cheeks will appear swollen and sore.

The solution is quite simple: the teeth will need clipping. In the first instance, it is best to refer the rat to your vet, who will clip the teeth down and prescribe antibiotics to reduce any infection caused by swelling of the penetrated areas. Obviously, if the cause of the teeth being overgrown is purely dietary or the lack of gnawing material, this is easily rectified in the future. If, however, malocclusion is the cause, the teeth will grow back again, but still will be misshapen, in which case they will need regular clipping. With a little practice, it is possible to learn to do this yourself, using special clippers or even strong nail clippers. It certainly will not hurt the rat if carried out carefully. The ultimate option is to ask your vet to remove the rat's incisor teeth. Rats have a set of molar teeth, which are quite sufficient for chewing purposes. However, whether or not your rat may cope with this change depends on the rat. After clipping or removal of severely overgrown teeth, the rat's mouth may be a little tender for a few days and the jaw muscles somewhat out of practice, making it difficult for the rat to eat. Give it moistened food or bread and water for

Close-up of a rat kitten being hand reared by the use of a doll's bottle. (The spout is an empty piece of wire insulator cover.)

a day or two, but coax it back onto harder food as soon as possible, to get its jaw working again and, of course, to hone down the teeth, which will have started to grow again.

TOOTH ABSCESSES

Occasionally, rats do suffer from infected tooth roots. An abscess usually swells up in the infected area of gum and is noticeable as a lump, most often situated under one of the eyes. Take your rat to the vet to have the abscess punctured and the pus drained off. In very severe cases, the tooth itself may have to be removed.

TUMOURS

Rats are, unfortunately, very susceptible to tumours, especially in later life. Tumours can appear in two forms: benign and malignant. Benign tumours are generally harmless, being quite soft to the touch. It is possible to put one's fingers around the tumour and touch the fingers together, as the tumour will not be attached to any underlying bodily tissues. Benign tumours can, however, grow very large and painful if untreated. The tumour can be surgically removed by a vet and, on most occasions, the rat will make a full recovery. However, having suffered from a tumour once, it is quite possible that a rat will develop further tumours. If the rat is elderly, it is kindest not to subject it to stressful surgery. If the tumours cause it discomfort, it may be kindest to have the rat put to sleep.

Malignant tumours are faster growing than benign tumours. They are hard to the touch and are attached to underlying bodily tissues. They can occur basically

anywhere on an afflicted rat, the most common areas being the flanks, stomach, throat and under the armpits. They are, of course, cancerous and have a terribly debilitating effect on the rat. There is no kindness in having such tumours removed, as the cancer will spread and will have already affected other parts of the rat's body anyway. The rat will suffer a good deal of discomfort, so it is best to have it put to sleep. Quite often, tumours are genetic in origin, so if you have a bloodline that is prone to tumours, it is best to discontinue the line.

TAPEWORMS

Normally, fancy rats should not suffer from tapeworms (of which there are several different species), as these are transmitted by wild rats' fleas. This situation might, however, arise in the case of an outdoor rattery that is "invaded" by wild rats. Signs of tapeworm infection are small rice-like particles in the rats' droppings. Cat tapeworm medication can be used successfully to treat this condition, but it would be on the safe side to refer the affected rats to a vet, who would probably prescribe a better tapeworm treatment. Rat-borne tapeworms of the *Hymenolepsis* genus can infect humans, so, if in doubt, visit your own doctor!

THE OLD RAT

Rats do have a rather short life, which is a great pity, as they are such engaging, lively animals. The average lifespan is between two and three years. Certainly, there are exceptions to the rule, and cases of rats dying at the ripe old age of five years have been recorded. If a rat does live beyond three years, it will undoubtedly look every day of its senior years and be somewhat slower in its actions.

An old rat sleeps more

A Dove Hooded rat. The life span of a rat averages between two and three years.

than it used to, avoids fights and confrontations with others (although it will have a shorter temper), and will be less playful. It will probably eat less and drink more, as its kidneys may be less effective than before. Elderly does cease to be

A very elderly rat, rather infirm and listless.

fertile, although elderly bucks may still think they have great sexual prowess and are irresistible to younger does. It may well be that an elderly buck *is* still fertile, but it is best not to use him for breeding, as the strain may be too great for his heart.

Elderly rats should not be taken to shows, as this is an extremely stressful event for them, even if they were used to it in younger life.

Being elderly, they are more prone to heart failure caused by stress and will easily catch colds and other infections. Basically, treat an elderly rat as you would treat an elderly human being: give them plenty of peace and quiet, a good diet, warm, dry conditions and plenty of gentle, restrained affection. It is a good idea to remove very high perches and swings in an old rat's cage, as its balance will not be as good as it once was, not that it would want to go clambering high up if it was a very tottery rat.

Much as you love your pet rat, or any other pet for that matter, when it becomes very old, the main thing to keep in mind is its *quality of life*. If the animal is in any pain or distress or is simply not enjoying life any more, it is best to have it put to sleep. This, of course, is a very traumatic decision for most people, but if you truly love and care about your pet, you owe it this final act of kindness. Having said that, the day may not come for euthanasia. Many rats die in their sleep, quite painlessly and in the environment that they have known and enjoyed throughout their lifetimes. However, euthanasia is one thing that every pet owner must have in mind, should such a day occur when their pet's quality of life has deteriorated markedly so as to make the pet miserable.

By and large, rats are fairly hardy little animals.

EUTHANASIA

Apart from the concept of culling, an elderly or terminally sick rat can be put to sleep by either of two effective, painless methods. The first is to simply take the rat to a vet. The vet will give the rat an injection in its side. All the rat will feel is the initial slight pain of the needle pricking its skin, but this will soon disappear as the rat drifts off to sleep. Basically, the vet will have given the rat an overdose of anesthetic, which just sends it into a deep sleep and eventually stops the heart from working. This method is a very gentle, kind way of allowing the rat to die in its sleep.

The second method is best if you cannot get to a vet at the time that you need him or if you keep a lot of rats and would need to be well versed in euthanasia. The method involves the use of ether or chloroform. Place the rat in a sealed container, in which you will then place a wad of tissue or a piece of cotton wool *soaked* in ether or chloroform. The rat may struggle a little to start with, but will quickly fall asleep. Leave it in the container for fifteen minutes to half an hour, by which time it will have fallen asleep and died painlessly.

Check that the rat is dead simply by checking that it is not breathing and that its heart has stopped beating. The heartbeat can be checked by placing your fingertip on the rat's left side, immediately under its foreleg. If the rat has been suffering from anything infectious, dispose of the body carefully, disinfect the cage and burn all sawdust, bedding and cage furniture that cannot be disinfected. Ensure also that you have a good wash, preferably using disinfectant on your hands.

By and large, rats are healthy animals. You don't need to be constantly worried about your rat's health, but daily care and observation are your best tools against preventing any ailments' getting a grip on him.

Healthy, active rats will enjoy cage accessories that allow them to exercise.

Varieties

As fancy rats have gained popularity, both as pets and exhibition animals, the number of different varieties in which they are available has increased. Many of the original fancy varieties bred by rat fanciers between the start of the rat fancy in 1901 and its official demise in 1931 had been lost for many years, but have since been re-discovered with the formation of the National Fancy Rat Society and the new rat fancy. In addition, having made a close study of the history of the varieties, I can categorically state that even more varieties have been developed since 1976 than ever existed previously. The curly-coated Rex, developed by Roy Robinson, is a good case in point, although Robinson had, of course, been working on developing this variety for several years prior to the formation of the N.F.R.S. in 1976.

A Champagne Rex rat. In its formative years, the rat fancy was to be foundly solely in England. Now it enjoys popularity in several different countries.

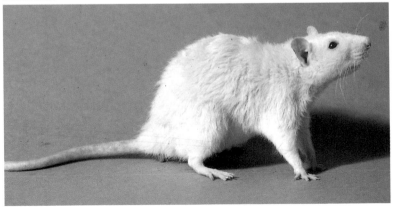

A Rex rat. If you look closely, you will see that the whiskers are curled as well.

One factor that has helped the speedier development of varieties in the modern rat fancy is that the fancy is spread into several different countries nowadays, whereas previously it had been confined to Great Britain. Although there have been a number of exports of British fancy rats to other countries, independent development of varieties has taken place, particularly in the United States. What often causes confusion in the development of any fancy livestock is the fact that the same varieties can be given different names in different countries. For

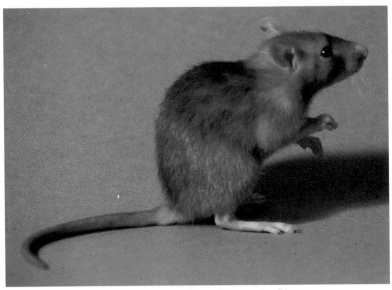

This is one of the newest color variants in rats: the Blue.

instance, with cats, *Colourpoint Persians*, first recognised in the U.K., are called *Himalayans* in the U.S. The British *Red Point Colourpoint* is known as the *Flame Point Himalayan* in the U.S. Possibly, the situation is a little better in the rat fancy, as rats are still rats, but whereas the prefix adjective "fancy" is applied in Britain and the U.S., there is no such word in Swedish, so fancy rats are termed "tamrattor" (literally "tame rats") in Scandinavia. With regard to the actual varieties, there are thankfully very few deviations from the original British variety names (or standards of excellence) to give them their proper description. One example of a different variety name

A Mink Capped rat. The blaze on this rat's forehead is "open." Ideally, the blaze should be closed.

being applied is the *Silver Fawn*. In America only, it is known as *Amber*, although the Amber is basically a pale, rather washed-out Silver Fawn. There is a genuine difference in the case of the *Berkshire* and *Irish.* In Britain, the Berkshire is described as of any standard colour with as much white on the chest as possible. The *American Berkshire* is described as having a far greater spread of white colouration on its underside. The *Irish,* possibly one of the oldest breeds, is described in the N.F.R.S. Standards as being of a standard colour with an equilateral triangle of white fur on its chest. In America, the Irish resembles what would be termed a very poorly marked Berkshire in Britain. The real confusion starts when the American fancy stages classes for both American-bred rats and British stock. This leads to the two varieties being described as *English Berkshire* and, most bizarre of all, *English Irish,* which conjours up visions of immigrant ancestors from the old countries settling in the New World in the mid 1800s or thereabouts!

Anyway, the main point is, differences *do* occur in some instances. I'm not going to stick my neck out and say what I, personally, think is correct or not. All that I will say on the subject is that, in the main, the British standards are *genetically* correct. Obviously, when the first rat

A mink rat.

A Silver Fawn Hooded rat. This rat's hood is rather uneven and blends into the saddle.

standards were prepared by the N.M.R.C. at the turn of the century, genetics was a largely unknown science that was not applied in any great detail to fancy livestock until much later. (The famous fancier H.C. Brooke used genetical information to classify his fancy *Rattus rattus* specimens.) This explains why some of the variety names were changed by the N.F.R.S. when their true genetical identities were discovered. There are a few varieties that are named more for the colour they resemble in other species of fancy livestock, although their genetical identity may be different.

GENERAL CONFORMATION

Before we examine each variety in greater detail, it is

essential to be aware of general conformation. Before any fancy rat is judged after its own standard, it is checked by the judge to see whether it meets the basic requirements of a good fancy rat. These requirements are mostly self-evident, such as being in possession of all four limbs, two eyes and two ears. General health and condition are considered, with certain health criteria being listed as disqualifying faults. By the very nature of its being a domesticated animal, any fancy rat should be tame and easily handled. Intractability can also disqualify a rat, no matter how good its colour or markings. All fancy rats must "look the part." Thin, scrawny, sharp-snouted specimens are not desired, nor indeed are any obese, lethargic animals. To this end, like all fancy livestock, fancy rats have to conform in terms of *type*. This is basically the required physical shape and carriage of the rat, which, if observed correctly, is a joy to behold in a well-typed specimen. Size and physique are also considered, all as part of the general conformation. Obviously, the finer points of ensuring rats with good size and type as well as good varieties must be carefully considered when breeding them.

The general conformation of a fancy rat, as laid down by the National Fancy Rat Society reads as follows:

"The rat shall be of good size, does long and racy in type, bucks being of a bigger build, arched over the loin, firm fleshed with clean, long head, but not too pointed at the nose. The eyes shall be round, bold, clean and of good size. The ears shall be of good size, well formed and widely spaced. The tail shall be cylindrical and as long as the body, thick at the base, tapering to a fine point. The ears, feet and tail shall be covered with fine hair. The coat shall be

A very unstandardised variety of rat: the "Blazed Berkshire," or Badger, rat.

smooth and glossy (except the Rex type). Bucks are larger than does and have a harsher coat."

Serious Faults

Serious faults include the following: poor condition or health, bare areas, scaliness of ears and/or kinked or short tail.

Disqualifying Faults

Disqualifying faults are as follows: lack of whiskers, severe scabs, mites and fleas, obvious ill-health, and intractability. (Taken from the N.F.R.S. Standards Of Excellence, December, 1986, © N.F.R.S.)

A Pink Eyed White (albino). It is this variety of rat that is commonly used in laboratory research.

The general conformation reads basically the same in all countries, allowing for all the major points to be considered.

VARIETIES

Now we turn to the individual varieties of fancy rats. I have deliberately listed only the British standards, correct at the time of writing, for two simple reasons. Firstly, as stated above, there are a number of varieties that go under different names in different countries, either due to translation, grammar or individual preference. In some countries, there are even differences of opinion within the fancy over the names or standards of each variety. For instance, in the United States, where there are at least five rat fancy organisations, the standards do, in many cases, vary in different degrees. To list them all would be extremely confusing for any reader, not to mention pointless to readers in countries where the varying standards do not apply. The second reason is simply space— there's just not enough

A Siamese rat. Note how the dark colouration extends well up into the hindquarters.

pages to cover all the variations of standards. If the reader wishes to study the standards in greater detail and compare any differences, then the best thing to do is to obtain a list of the standards of excellence from each society or group. Obviously, no standards for *Rattus rattus* have been drawn up, although the original 1920s standards still exist for reference, should *Rattus rattus* ever make a fancy comeback.

An explanatory note about the way in which the N.F.R.S. Standards are grouped. This basically follows the schedule of classes to which rats are judged in the U.K. Self-coloured rats are grouped as Dark Eyed or Pink Eyed, Marked Varieties are grouped together, although judged separately. The notes on the origins of each variety are purely my own and do not form an integral part of the published standards.

STANDARDS OF EXCELLENCE © N.F.R.S. 1986/1991

Self—Dark Eyed

BLACK EYED WHITE: To be as white as possible, devoid of creamy tinge or staining. Any coloured hairs to be severely penalised. Eyes black.

Points for Black Eyed White:

Colour of eye—Black: 20 points

Coat colour—White, no dark hairs or patches: 30 points

Remainder—General Conformation: 50 points

Total: 100 points

Origins:

Bred in *Rattus rattus* fancy species by H.C. Brooke circa 1915. Good fancy specimens shown in 1919/20. Re-introduced (in *Rattus norvegicus*) by Rosemary and Pat Quaid and Diane Wildman (U.K.) in 1984. Full standardisation granted in 1986.

BLACK: To be a deep, solid black, devoid of dinginess and white hairs or patches. Base fur to be black. Foot colour to match top. Eyes black.

MINK: To be an even mid grey-brown, devoid of dinginess, silvering or patches and having a distinct bluish sheen. Foot colour to match top. Eyes black.

CHOCOLATE: To be a deep, rich chocolate, as even as possible, devoid of dinginess and white hairs or patches. Foot colour to match top. Eyes black.

Points for Self Black, Mink and Chocolate:

Top Colour: 20 points

Belly colour—to match top colour: 10 points

Feet (5 points per foot): 20 points

Remainder—General Conformation: 50 points

Total: 100 points

Origins:

BLACK: One of the earliest colour mutations, occuring in the wild in melanistic characteristic. Was being shown from start of N.M.R.C. rat fancy circa

1901. As with all self coloured rats, Blacks are prone to silvering to various degrees. Separate silver standards provided for such specimens, by both N.M.R.C. and N.F.R.S.

MINK: Originally listed as "Blue" (circa 1905?). Bred as Mink by Genesis Stud (U.K.). Into N.F.R.S. Standards 1977. There is still a lot of experimentation going on with this breed, which is part of the "Blue" series. It is highly likely that *Lilac* (as yet unstandardised) is a variant of Mink, with extra white diluting the overall colour.

CHOCOLATE: First bred circa 1915. In standards by 1935. Carried forward to N.F.R.S. Standards 1976, deleted from same in 1978, as no specimens had been shown. Reintroduced by Chriss Lown (U.K.) 1981. Full standardisation 1983.

Self—Pink Eyed

CHAMPAGNE: To be an evenly warm beige, with no suggestion of dullness or greyness. Eyes red.

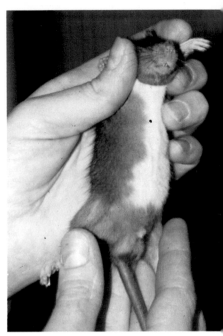

A Berkshire rat showing white belly markings.

PINK EYED WHITE: To be as white as possible, devoid of creamy tinge or staining. Eyes pink.

Points for Champagne and Pink Eyed White:

Top colour: 25 points

Belly colour—to match top colour, no thin patches: 25 points

Remainder—General Conformation: 50 points
Total: 100 points
Origins:

CHAMPAGNE: Possibly classed as "Cream" circa 1935 standards. In N.F.R.S. Standards as Champagne 1976. (Cream deleted from N.F.R.S. Standards 1978—no specimens bred.)

Pink Eyed White (Albino): Said by Mary Douglas to be introduced into Britain from a pair obtained in France by a travelling showman early in the nineteenth century. However, very likely bred before this date, being the commonest form of wild mutation. In standards 1901. Carried forward to N.F.R.S. Standards, 1976.

Marked Varieties

BERKSHIRE: To be symmetrically marked, with as much white on the chest and belly as possible. The white shall not extend up the sides of the body, the edges shall be clear cut and devoid of brindling. Back feet to be white to the ankle, forelegs to be white to half the leg. Tail to be white to half its length. The body colour shall conform to a recognised colour variety. The white area shall be pure and devoid of any colour or staining. A white spot on the forehead is desirable. Points for Berkshire:

Top colour: 15 points
Belly markings: 15 points
Tail stop: 10 points
Foot stops: 5 points
Head spot: 5 points
Remainder—General Conformation: 50 points
Total: 100 points
Origins:

Introduced circa 1957. Name said to be based on the same name given to a breed of marked pig. Carried through all standards to 1976.

IRISH: White equilateral triangle on chest with front feet white and back feet white to half their length. The triangle to be of good size, clear cut and devoid of brindling, not to extend in a streak down the belly but to

A Black Variegated rat. The variegation should be as even and widespread on the rat's body as possible.

occupy all the space between the front legs. The body colour shall conform to a recognised colour variety.

Points for Irish:
Triangle: 20 points
Top colour: 15 points
Foot stops: 10 points
Belly colour: 5 points
Remainder—General Conformation: 50 points
Total: 100 points
Origins:
Said by Mary Douglas to resemble a *Rattus rattus* sub-species, *Mus Hibernicus*, found on coasts of Ireland by a Mr. Thompson in 1837, said sub-species having a white diamond or triangle marking on its chest. A black *Mus Hibernicus* was shown by Mr. Vale at the very first rat show in Aylesbury in 1901, and was placed 4th. A good fancy specimen was shown by a Mr. Halling in 1906. In standards as Irish by 1907. Standard carried forward to

An Agouti Hooded rat. Note the straight saddle line extending down the back.

1976. (Known in America as "English Irish," to differentiate from "American" Irish, which resembles a Berkshire with less white than usual).

HOODED: The hood shall be unbroken, covering the head, throat, chest and shoulders, except in the case of light coloured hooded varieties where a pale coloured throat and chest is permissible. The hood shall be continuous with the saddle, extending down the spine to the tail with as much of the tail as possible being coloured. The saddle width shall be ¼ to ½ an inch in width (nearer ¼")—it must be as even as possible and unbroken. The edges of the hood and saddle shall be clear cut and devoid of brindling. The white area shall be pure and devoid of yellow tinge or staining.

Points for Hooded:

Saddle: 15 points

Colour of Hood and Saddle: 10 points

Colour of white parts—no spots or staining: 10 points

Hood: 10 points

Tail: 5 points

Remainder—General Conformation: 50 points

Total: 100 points

Origins:

Introduced in basic form as "Even Marked" circa 1901, possibly earlier. (Jack Black and Jimmy Shaw bred "Pied" rats circa 1840/50). In standard as "Even Marked" 1901. Amended to "Japanese" by 1915. In standards as "Japanese Hooded" 1957. In N.F.R .S. Standards as "English Hooded" 1976. Referred to as "Hooded" by 1977 and onwards. A variant of Hooded has been developed in the U.S.A., known as *Bareback*, a Hooded rat without a saddle, originally bred from

The Lilac. It is highly improbable that a self version of this colour will ever exist, as the white fur dilutes the main body colour from Mink to Lilac.

Hooded stock by Karla Barber.

CAPPED: The colour not to extend past the ears and to follow the line of the lower jaw bone, it should not extend under the chin. A white blaze or spot on the face, and the rest of the body white. Colour to conform to a recognised colour variety. White area should be pure and devoid of yellowish tinge or staining.

Points for Capped:
Cap: 20 points
Body colour: 15 points
Blaze (or spot): 10 points
(Open blazes to be penalised by a maximum of 5 points.)
Colour of Cap: 5 points
Remainder—General Conformation: 50 points
Total: 100 points
Origins:

Introduced as "Dutch Headed Even" by H.C. Brooke, circa 1915. Said via *Fur & Feather* article (1909) that such rats had been bred in the 1860s (not verified). Carried through standards as "Dutch." Re-introduced in more familiar form as "Hooded" by Mrs. J. Curzon, circa 1962, later re-named "Capped." Re-introduced by Les Suttling (U.K.) 1976/77. Fully standardised by 1981.

VARIEGATED: The head and shoulders to be of any distinct colour, with a white blaze on the forehead. The variegation to cover the body from the shoulders to the tail including the sides. The colour to conform to a recognised colour variety. Belly colour to be white, devoid of creamy tinge or staining.

Points for Variegated:
Variegation: 25 points
Colour: 10 points
Blaze: 5 points
Tail—variegated: 5 points
Hood: 5 points
Remainder—General Conformation: 50 points
Total: 100 points
Origin:

Bred as "Broken Marked" circa 1900. In standards by 1909, but to be bred/shown without hood. Bred as "Variegated" by Mr. Butler-Adams 1921, but remained in standards as "Broken Marked" circa 1935. Reintroduced as "Variegated" by Les Suttling 1977. Second reintroduction by Jean Judd 1981 (U.K.) Full standardisation granted to both fanciers in 1984.

Silver Varieties

SILVER: To be of a recognised coat colour, the

A Silver Grey rat. Note the silvered guard hairs, known as "ticking."

coat containing equal numbers of silver and non-silver guard hairs. Each silver hair to have as much of its length white as possible—a coloured tip to be allowed. Silvering to give an overall sparkling appearance. It should not be possible to confuse a Silver with a Pearl or a Self. Foot color to match top. *NB:* Silver Blacks are to be known as "Silver Grey."

Points for Silver Agouti and Cinnamon:

Top colour including head: 30 points

Belly colour—as per Agouti and Cinnamon Standards: 10 points

Feet : 10 points

Remainder—General Conformation: 50 points

Total: 100 points

Points for Silver Grey, Mink and Chocolate:

Top colour including head: 30 points

Belly colour—to match top

colour: 10 points
    Feet: 10 points
    Remainder—General
Conformation: 50 points
    Total: 100 points
    Origins:

All rats are silvered to a greater or lesser extent, this trait not being visible in very pale varieties, such as Pink Eyed White, as an extreme example. Prior to 1981, no formal provision had been made in any set of rat standards for any Silvered variety, except "Silver Grey." This variety was bred as such circa 1909. In standards by the mid 1920s. Listed in standards 1935. Introduced to N.F.R.S. Standards 1981, along with other Silvered varieties.

SILVER FAWN: To be a rich orange fawn, evenly ticked with silver guard hairs. Belly fur to be white, the demarcation between the top colour and white belly to be sharp and clear cut, devoid of irregularities and brindling. Eyes red.

    Points for Silver Fawn:
    Top colour: 15 points
    Ticking: 10 points
    Demarcation: 15 points
    Belly Colour: 10 points
    Remainder—General
Conformation: 50 points
    Total: 100 points
    Origins:

Bred originally as "Fawn" circa 1910. Bred and classified as Silver Fawn circa 1922. In standards 1935. Entered in N.F.R.S. Standards as "Argente" in 1976, amended to "Silver Fawn Argente" then finally "Silver Fawn" soon after.

This variety is shown under various names in various shades in the U.S.A., including "Orange Fawn" and "Amber." In the U.K., the Silver Fawn is one of the most popular varieties and has won more Best In Shows and top awards than any other variety.

Other Varieties

AGOUTI: To be a rich, ruddy brown, evenly ticked with black guard hairs. Base fur dark grey to black. Belly fur to be silver grey. Foot colour to match top. Eyes black.

A Cinnamon Pearl. A good specimen of rat will have eyes that are round, bold, clean, and of good size.

CINNAMON: To be a warm russet brown, evenly ticked with chocolate guard hairs. Base fur mid-grey. Belly fur as Agouti but of a lighter shade. Foot colour to match top. Eyes black. Points for Agouti and Cinnamon:

Top colour: 15 points

Ticking: 10 points
Belly colour : 10 points
Undercoat: 5 points
Feet: 10 points
Remainder—General Conformation: 50 points
Total: 100 points
Origins:
AGOUTI: First shown at Cheltenham by Douglas and

Vale, 1902. In standards as such circa 1902. Carried through all standards to 1976. Although often thought to be the same colour as the wild rat, the fancy Agouti is much redder.

CINNAMON: Introduced as "Fawn Agouti" circa mid 1920s. In 1935 standards as such. Renamed in N.F.R.S. Standards as Cinnamon in 1976.

HIMALAYAN: Body colour to be white, free from stains and even throughout. The points to be a rich dark sepia (as dark as possible). Eyes red. Note—Colour areas: 1. Face—not to extend upwards from eyes. 2. Ears—not to extend downwards from the base. 3. Forelegs—not to extend upwards beyond the elbows. 4. Hind legs—not to extend upwards beyond the ankle. 5 Tail—not to extend beyond the tail root. 6. Feet—colour to be solid throughout, devoid of any white.

Points for Himalayan:
Body colour—white, including belly: 20 points
Feet—sepia brown: 10 points
Tail: 10 points
Nose and ears: 10 points
Remainder—General Conformation: 50 points
Total: 100 points
Origins:
Himalayan is a variety that never existed in the old rat fancy. There is, however, some evidence that a form of Himalayan was bred during the 1950s "Rat Revival". It was bred in basic form in a laboratory in Orly, France, circa 1972. Imported by geneticist Roy Robinson (U.K.) 1978. N.F.R.S. Standard drawn up 1978. Full standardisation 1981.

SIAMESE: Body colour to be medium beige gradually and evenly shaded over saddle and hindquarters towards the belly, being darkest at the base of the tail. There should be no white or very pale areas anywhere on the body, feet or tail. Belly to be light beige. Points to be rich dark sepia and to shade evenly into the body colour. Eyes ruby.

Points for Siamese:
Shading: 20 points
Colour of points: 15 points
Colour of body: 15 points
Remainder—General Conformation: 50 points
Total: 100 points

Origins:
Bred from Himalayan circa 1979. Full standardisation 1981. This variety has enjoyed a very good show record worldwide, largely thanks to stock bred by Geoff Izzard.

PEARL: To be palest silver, shading to creamish undercolour. Each hair to

A Topaz rat (formerly Argente). In exhibition animals, the ears should be of good size and widely spaced.

be delicately tipped with grey evenly over the whole animal. Belly fur pale silver grey. Foot colour to match top. Eyes black.

Points for Pearl:
Top colour: 25 points
Belly colour: 15 points
Feet: 10 points
Remainder—General Conformation: 50 points
Total: 100 points
Origins:

Another variety that did not exist (as far as can be ascertained) in the old rat fancy. Bred simultaneously by Clive Love of Genesis Stud (U.K.) and Jackie Chapman (U.K.) in 1978. The Pearl was bred out of pale Mink. Provisional standardisation granted to Jackie Chapman. Full standardisation 1981.

CINNAMON PEARL: Coat to consist of three (3) bands of colour from the base up—cream, blue and orange, with silver guard hairs, to give an overall golden appearance with a silver sheen. Belly fur pale silver grey. Foot colour to match top. Eyes black.

Points for Cinnamon Pearl:
Top colour: 15 points
Ticking: 10 points
Feet: 10 points
Belly: 10 points
Base coat—cream: 5 points
Remainder—General Conformation: 50 points
Total : 100 points
Origins:

There is no previous reference to any variety resembling Cinnamon Pearl prior to 1979. By incredible coincidence, it was bred simultaneously once again by Clive Love (Genesis Stud) and Jackie Chapman in 1979. Provisional and Full standardisation granted to Genesis Stud in 1979 and 1982 respectively.

Coat Varieties

REX: The coat to be evenly dense and not excessively harsh, with as few guard hairs as possible. Coat to be evenly curled and also to a lesser extent on the belly. Curly vibrissae (whiskers) are normal for

A Black Eyed White. For those who love the white coat of the albino but not the pink eyes, this variety is an attractive alternative.

Rex. Colour to conform to a recognised colour or pattern variety. Where silver or ticked rats are rexed, allowances should be made for the lower number of guard hairs present than in normal varieties.

Points for Rex:
Colour/Pattern/Condition: 30 points

Body, type and size: 15 points

Fur: 30 points
Head: 5 points
Eyes: 5 points
Tail: 5 points
Ears: 5 points
Feet: 5 points
Total: 100 points
Origins:
Bred by Roy Robinson, geneticist (U.K.) 1976. Into N.F.R.S. Standards 1976.

NOTE: Where reference is made to the 1935

You can train your rat to stand up when you want it to by offering it a treat.

Standards, these are the rat standards then in use for the limited number of rats shown at that time, compiled and updated by the National Mouse Club.

THE STANDARDISATION PROCEDURE EXPLAINED

At the time of writing, there are a number of new varieties that have not, as yet, been granted standards. Some of these varieties have a long way to go before standardisation can be contemplated; to achieve this status, the variety must *breed true*: that is, a rat of a given colour, mated to the same colour, will produce offspring of the same colour. The variety must also be judged at several shows by different judges who adjudge it to be an accurate representation of whatever variety the breeder says it to be. Usually, some form of *guide standard* is drawn up for a new variety, so that judges can at least refer to what the breeder is aiming to achieve in the variety. As I remarked earlier, in many cases of "invented" varieties, it would be well-nigh impossible to follow the procedure of breeding true, showing well, and producing a guide standard.

In the N.F.R.S., the procedure toward standardisation is not a quick and easy route, but ultimately one that works.

A trio of fancy rats at play.

The initial guide standard is drawn up between the breeder and standards officer of the society and is given approval by the committee. The variety is then judged according to the guide standard. If after an indeterminate period the variety is felt to be progressing, a *provisional standard* will be drawn up, with any amendments to the initial guide standard duly made. To all intents and purposes, the provisional standard is exactly the same as a full standard, but is reviewed after a fixed period of time, usually two years. If in the opinion of the judges the variety has progressed and shown well, the matter is considered by the standards officer and committee. The standard will then be granted full status and will ultimately be verified by the society's membership at a general meeting. But it isn't always as easy as that in every case. For instance, the Variegated was developed independently by two fanciers—Les Suttling and Jean Judd, some years apart. The provisional standard was granted in 1981, but given an additional year's "probation" in 1983. It finally achieved full status in 1984. The Black Eyed White, on the other hand, sailed through the procedure within two years, between 1984 and 1986. Generally speaking, the more complex the variety—physically and genetically—the harder it will be to achieve

A line-up of show tanks, with their occupants awaiting their turns to be judged.

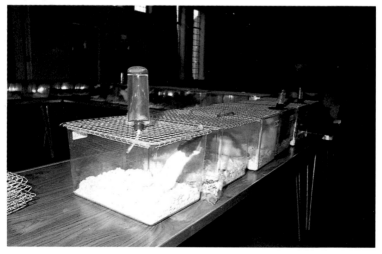

standardisation. In any case, everything depends on the dedication of a handful, or often, individual, fanciers who persevere to breed that new variety over a number of years.

UNSTANDARDISED VARIETIES

The *Lilac* has been around for many years and is still unstandardised. A great deal of of work has been put into this breed by a number of fanciers, but the genetical formula is quite complex. To date, work continues on the Lilac. If nothing else, the Lilac is a very attractive variety, being a pleasing shade of light grey, often with a good amount of white blending into the overall colour.

The *Blue* was discovered in a litter of kittens in a pet shop in 1990 by Roger and Joan Branton of the N.F.R.S. Nothing was known about the background of the kittens, which the Brantons eagerly bought, but remarkably,

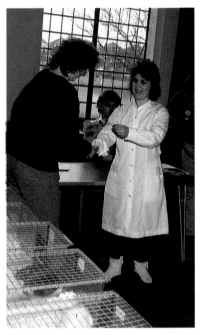

A successful exhibitor claims her prize at the end of a show.

they bred true. Theoretically, from Blue, varieties such as Blue Agouti, Opal and Lynx could one day be developed. Only time will tell. As yet, no guide standard exists, although several fanciers have taken up the gauntlet of breeding and developing this most attractive variety, surely one of the most exciting developments standard-wise for many years. In the late 1980s, I am proud to say, I was instrumental in importing the forerunners to three new varieties to England from America, initially via Sweden!

Beige and *Fawn* rats had been exported to Sweden by the American Fancy Rat and Mouse Association, and these two varieties had proved to be fairly popular. When my wife Marianne moved to England, we imported a lot of her animals, which then had to spend time in quarantine. Amongst the rats were a few mismarked Berkshires, which were "carriers" of the Fawn and Beige. Whilst in quarantine, these rats bred, producing the first U.K.-

Rats should be kept in adequately sized accommodations, whether you have only one rat or several.

One of the most exciting aspects of the fancy is the potential for developing new color varieties.

bred Fawns and Beiges. These were then released to interested breeders to take up. A few months later, some genuine American Beiges were imported and bred in with the British stock. By now it had become clear that the Beiges were developing into two distinct varieties—one darker than the other. Initially, these were named *Dove* and *Dark Eyed Champagne*. The Fawns were identified as Argentes. In time, more American Argentes were imported, courtesy of Dr. Ed Friedlander, a noted scientist, and again, they were used in the breeding programme. British fanciers Rosemary and Pat Quaid had independently bred their own version of this variety, named "Dark Eyed Silver Fawn." These were later absorbed into the Argente breeding programme. At the time of writing, two of the three varieties have received guide standards, namely *Buff* (formerly Dark Eyed Champagne) and *Topaz* (formerly Argente). The

Dove, which has not proved quite as popular (or easy to breed) as its lighter Buff counterpart, is still being bred and developed.

The guide standards for Buff and Topaz, as drawn up by the National Fancy Rat Society © 1991 are as follows:

BUFF: To be an even, warm magnolia, with no sign of dullness or greyness. Belly colour to match top. Eyes to be dark ruby.

Points for Buff:
Top Colour: 25 points
Belly colour—to match top colour: 15 points
Eye colour: 10 points
Remainder—General Conformation: 50 points
Total: 100 points

TOPAZ: To be a rich, golden fawn evenly ticked with silver guard hairs. Undercolour to be pale blue/grey carried down to the skin. Belly fur to be silver. Top colour to be even and carried well down the sides with a clear differentiation between belly and top colour. Any tendency to sootiness or greyness of the top colour to be penalised. Eyes to be dark ruby.

Points for Topaz:
Top colour: 20 points
Ticking: 10 points
Undercolour: 5 points
Belly colour: 5 points
Eye colour: 10 points
Remainder—General Conformation: 50 points
Total: 100 points

So, there you have them—the varieties of fancy rat. No doubt many others will be discovered in time...Maybe the elusive Longhair, or even the Rosetted! Who knows? Maybe *you* will be the originator of a new variety!

Exhibiting

The logical progression for the rat fancier, now fully acquainted with the standards of the different varieties of rats, is that of actually exhibiting rats at a show. Sometimes, the prospect of entering and attending a show causes some folk unnecessary worry and concern. The most frequent comments that I have heard on this subject, for example, are: "I don't understand what all these different classes

Judging gets underway at a show. English rat judge Kandice Threapleton is explaining the fine points of the exhibits to an attentive trainee judge.

mean—which of them applies to my rats?" and "What sort of cage do I show my rats in?" or, one of the most regular worries; "How do I prepare my rats for a show?" Well, the object of this chapter is to help the prospective exhibitor get over some of these fears; the whole process of exhibiting fancy rats, from the initial selection of show stock to actually attending the show isn't half as terrifying or complicated as it may, at first, seem. As is to be expected, rat societies and clubs in different countries stage their shows in slightly different ways. It would, of course, be far too confusing to explain all the differences in procedure in one chapter, so I have based my explanation around a typical

Size and overall conformation are important considerations in assessing the quality of a show rat.

Even a mismarked rat like this little chap can enter a rat show in the pet class.

show staged by the British National Fancy Rat Society and other typical British groups. Any *major* points of differing procedures (i.e., the use of standardised show pens) are explained in the course of the chapter. So, now to discover the joys and delights of the rat show!

SELECTING SHOW STOCK

Having decided that you are going to attend a given show, the first, logical step is to select which rats you are going to exhibit (show). Of course, if you only have a couple of rats, then your choice is easier. If you have a larger stud, then careful selection is required. It is no good entering as many rats as possible for whatever reason—to increase your chances of winning or to boost the show's entry. If the rats you enter are not of good show quality, then they will be judged accordingly, and it will not increase your chances of winning. To load a show with sub-standard rats will only waste the judge's time, possibly even allowing him or her to have less time to spend judging really worthwhile rats. As a judge myself, I would much rather judge a show consisting of forty-odd rats of good quality than eighty-plus, half of which are mediocre or poor quality. So, in short, careful selection of your show stock is required. The logical guide for suitable show stock, is, of course, the general conformation, followed by the individual standard for the particular variety in question. Don't be swayed into showing any rat with bald patches, sores, spots or scabs, no matter

how perfect its colour or markings. Sneezing and wheezing rats most definitely are not to be considered, as indeed are any intractable specimens. Very young or old rats should not be shown, as the trauma of travelling and being at the show is very stressful for them. Obviously pregnant does should *never* be shown.

Sometimes, even the most experienced fanciers can suffer from "show blindness." A rat that has done well in any number of previous shows will not always be in top show condition. Sometimes it will be difficult to see a deterioration in its conformation, etc., especially in the context of your own stud, with no other specimens to judge it against, except your own. So, don't try to "overshow" a rat. The show life of rats is rather short, averaging about six months in total, after which time any good specimens should be used

The author and a show participant discussing her entry. Attending shows will give you a good idea of what constitutes a good specimen of a rat.

in your breeding programme. Make your selection carefully, in a considered manner. It will augur all the better for you at the show.

THE SHOW SCHEDULE

Most shows, when advertised, state what kind of *show schedule* is being used. The show schedule is the list of classes in which your rats may be entered. I have included a typical show schedule as used by the N.F.R.S. for most of its shows. A brief explanation of the different grades of classes are as follows:

Breed Classes: In this case, classes 1 to 38 inclusive. These are classes in which the rats will first be entered, by their variety. Odd-numbered classes apply to *adults*, even-numbered classes apply to *kittens* (between six and thirteen weeks of age).

Duplicate Classes: These classes are "secondary" classes, in which rats are entered in the normal way, but in which all different varieties are in competition with each other. The *Adult and Kitten Challenges* are classes in which the winners of the breed classes in each age group compete with each other for the top placings.

The winners in each of these challenges are then pitted against each other in the *Supreme Challenge*, whereby the very top placings in the show are judged: Best In Show, Best Opposite Age (i.e., if the Best In Show is an adult, the Best Opposite Age is the top kitten or vice-versa), and Reserve Best In Show (the second-highest placed rat, which need not necessarily be the Best Opposite Age Rat. In the case of B.I.S. and R.B.I.S. being awarded, both rats will be in the same age grouping. B.O.A. may be placed 3rd or even less in the Supreme Challenge, but will still apply the Best Rat in the opposite age grouping.).

Stud Buck is a class for adult bucks only and has no real bearing on results in the Challenges. The rats in this class are judged mainly on their size, type and general physique and desirability as the ideal "stud" rat. Of course, colour and markings are considered in the sense that a good stud buck must have decent variety traits to pass on, but this takes second place to general conformation and physique.

Juvenile is, as the explanation on the schedule says, a class for rats owned by exhibitors under 16 years of age. Placings in this class are made according to the rats' placings in the Challenges and/or breed classes.

A smooth coat with no bare spots is another important requirement for the show rat.

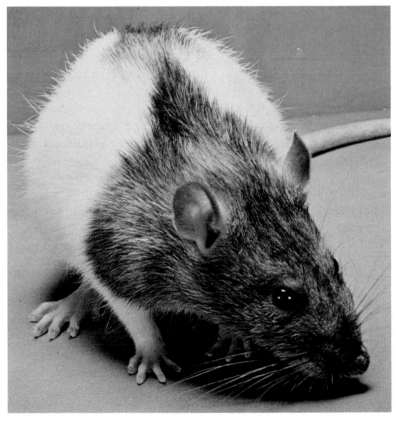

Pets: These classes are for non-show quality rats only. No rats entered in these classes may be entered elsewhere in the show. So, basically, even if your much loved pet rat is mis-marked or poorly coloured, it can still be shown as a pet. The judging in these classes is purely done on condition and tractability. A good starting ground for anybody wishing to progress into showing proper.

Unstandardised: A class for rats without an official standard (i.e., new varieties being developed, such as Dove or Lilac).

Guide Standard: A relatively new class for rats that have just achieved a guide standard but not full standardisation.

All shows staged by the N.F.R.S. have a *block entry* system in operation. This means that, for the set entry fee, your rat will be entered in *all* the classes for which it is eligible. To some extent, this takes the onus off the exhibitor for having to

A bath will help the show rat—as well as the pet-quality rat—to look its very best. Start by assembling the bathing equipment: a plastic wash bowl, filled to about 3 in. (7.5cm) with warm water, a mild animal shampoo, a toothbrush, and a towel.

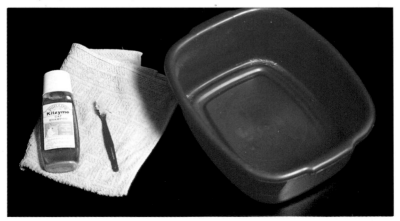

A TYPICAL RAT SHOW SCHEDULE

CLASS NO. ADULT	BREED CLASSES	CLASS NO. KITTEN
1	Black Eyed Self	2
3	Pink Eyed Self	4
5	Champagne	6
7	Any Other Colour Self	8
9	Hooded	10
11	Capped	12
13	Berkshire	14
15	Irish	16
17	Variegated	18
19	Rex A.C.A.V.	20
21	Silver Fawn	22
23	Silver Varieties (other than silver fawn)	24
25	Himalayan	26
27	Siamese	28
29	Agouti	30
31	Cinnamon	32
33	Pearl	34
35	Cinnamon Pearl	36
37	Guide Standard	38

	DUPLICATE CLASSES	
39	*Adult Challenge	
	*Kitten Challenge	40
41	*Supreme Challenge—A.V.A.A.	
42	*Stud Buck	
43	*Juvenile (Exhibitor must be under 16 years of age)	
44	Pets—Adult Exhibitor (Not entered in any other Class)	
45	Pets—Juvenile Exhibitor (Not entered in any other Class)	
46	Unstandardised (Not entered in any other Class)	

*Indicates entries must be duplicated (i.e., entered in Breed Class first).   © N.F.R.S. 1992

As you can see from the above show schedule, there are a number of options available when it comes to selecting which class (or classes) you want to enter.

decide which classes to enter. However, a good fancier should always *know* which classes any of his rats are entered in and *why*. Let us now turn to the actual process of making an entry in a show.

MAKING YOUR ENTRIES

Let's take as an example that you have three rats to enter in a show. These are: A *Silver Fawn Adult Buck*, a *Cinnamon Kitten* and a *Dove*.

First, taking the Silver Fawn, check which breed class number he is "classed under." He is an adult, so will be entered in *Class 21*—Silver Fawn Adult. Next, check the duplicate classes. Being an adult, he is to be entered in *Class 39* —Adult Challenge. He will, of course, be eligible for *Class 41*, the Supreme Challenge, listed as Any Variety, Any Age (A.V.A.A.). Now, checking a little further, being an adult buck, he is eligible to enter *Class 42*, the Stud Buck class. Are you a juvenile exhibitor? If

so, then *Class 43* is for your rat, too. He cannot enter Pets, as he is a show-quality Silver Fawn, and the Unstandardised class obviously doesn't apply to Silver Fawn.

Turning to the Cinnamon Kitten, by using the same process, it will be entered in *Breed Class 32*—Cinnamon Kitten, *Class 40*—Kitten Challenge and *Class 41*— Supreme Challenge. Again, assuming you remember that you are under 16 years of age, then *Class 43*— Juvenile, has a place for your kitten, too.

Finally, the Dove. This variety is currently Unstandardised, so there is only one class in which it can be entered: *Class 46*— Unstandardised.

The next step is to total up your entry fees and write or telephone your entries through to the show

Opposite page: Small and easily transportable, rats present no difficulties when it comes to traveling to shows.

Carefully introduce your rat to the bath water, gently reassuring it the whole time.

don't have any of your own. As far as I am aware, the N.F.R.S. is the only society that uses standardised show pens. These pens are actually small plastic aquariums, with specially made wire sliding lids. Not only does this procedure make things look much neater and professional at shows, it is easier for the stewards to fetch and carry the pens to the judge's table. It is fairer than the systems in some other countries, where the exhibitor brings his or her rat up to the judge. By using show tanks and stewards, the exhibitor is anonymous and the judge cannot be influenced in any way, thereby being able to concentrate on the task of judging the rats themselves.

PREPARING YOUR RATS FOR A SHOW

Fancy rats are, of course, naturally very clean creatures. However, with the best will in the world and even the most

secretary, being careful to enter within the specified time, before the closing date for entries. At the time of entry, you may need to hire some show pens, if you

Use one hand to restrain the rat in the bowl; use the other hand to gently soak him.

fastidious of cleaning habits, they can still get a bit grubby in their usual housing environment. In this case, it is always advisable to clean them up to some extent before a show. In this way, the rat will then show at its best, without any external blemishes spoiling its condition on the big day. Some rats, particularly pale varieties, may well need a bath before the show, as their coats often get stained. The bathtime procedure is fairly simple.

First, prepare the bath. Use a sink, basin or bowl, and place no more than three inches of lukewarm water in it. Next, gently place your rat in the water. At first, the rat may become a little panicky, so talk to it quietly and reassure it. Gently pour some water over its fur, using your hand or a small cup, whilst restraining the rat with your other hand, until its fur is completely wet. Next, apply some pet shampoo or a mild liquid cleanser to the fur. Just a little shampoo goes a long

Take care to avoid getting shampoo into the eyes and ears.

way, remember. Rub the shampoo into the coat, being careful to avoid the eyes and ears, until a good lather is built up. Next, rinse the shampoo away using fresh water. Sometimes, it is possible to carefully hold the rat under a tap, so long as the tap is of the mixer kind and is lukewarm or tepid!

Often, rats' tails get very dirty. There is a simple procedure for cleaning them. At the same time as the rat is being bathed, make sure that the tail is wet. Next, rub some soap, shampoo, or mild liquid cleanser into an old toothbrush. Now use the toothbrush to scrub the rat's tail. The dirt is then simply rubbed away. Be careful not to brush the tail too hard, as this will make it red and sore, and may even rub some of the natural scales away, thus "skinning" the tail, which is very painful for the rat.

With the ablutions now complete, you can dry the

After shampooing, be sure to thoroughly rinse off all lather.

rat, using either a towel to dry off the greater part of the fur and then leave the rat to wash itself down afterwards, or by carefully using a hairdryer, holding it sufficiently far away from the rat so as not to burn its skin. Whatever method you

Use a gentle rubbing action to remove excess water.

choose, make sure that the rat is dry to some extent, as it will easily catch cold if left wet. Be careful as to when you give a bath to a particular variety. Pale-coloured rats, such as Champagnes, Pink Eyed Whites, Himalayans, etc., should be bathed the night before a show, as they stain very easily. Darker varieties, such as Blacks and Minks should be bathed about a week prior to the show. This is because the bathing washes away a certain amount of the natural fats and oils in the fur, which give these varieties their lustrous, glossy sheen. Within a week, the natural

A brisk toweling down completes the bath routine.

oils will return to replace the veneer, so to speak.

Rexes, with their curly coats, should also be bathed about a week before a show, to allow for the fact that bathing makes them lose their curls temporarily. Within a week, the curls should return with no ill effect. Bucks of any variety tend to need bathing more often (before shows) than

does, as they have harsher fur that easily gets greasy.

Finally, check your rats' claws. Very often, judges can get scratched quite badly during the course of a show, handling so many rats. Therefore, it does no harm to trim your rats' claws before a show. Use a small nail clipper and simply clip off the tip of each claw. Be careful not to cut off too much and thus make the quick (the vein that runs through the claw) bleed. Rats have pale claws, so it should be easy to gauge exactly where to cut. Remember: "stick to the tip" and you won't go wrong.

Plucking of long guard hairs is frowned upon in some rat societies. My view is, by all means pluck a few maverick hairs, but don't make it *too* obvious that your rat has been plucked. Simple "tidying up" is one thing; altering a rat's appearance completely is quite another and will be treated with disqualification! Remember that a good judge will notice any obvious attempts to drastically alter a rat's appearance, so cheating just isn't worth it.

AT THE SHOW

So, you've reached the show. First of all, see the show secretary to pay for your entries and collect your pen labels, which indicate the number given to each exhibit. Do any last minute show preparation on your rats—perhaps using a bit of dog or cat stain remover on the coat, a quick brush down, etc. Now the exhibits must be placed in their show pens, ready for the stewards to put the classes in numerical order. The show will then get under way.

By all means, *talk* to people, *ask* questions, and *learn* what is going on. Of course, whilst judging is in progress, you may not talk to the judge, but any fancier will explain what's going on. In fact, one of the best ways to observe the judging at close quarters is to steward for the judge. So why not ask to be a steward? In fact, the stewards play an essential role in the smooth running of the show, and many top judges started their careers as stewards.

Opposite page: A job well done: one clean rat, ready for the show!

At the conclusion of the show, ask the judge his or her opinion of your rats, whether they have done well or not. By doing so, you will then learn whether or not you are heading in the right direction with your stock. Check any prize cards carefully. I always say that a well earned placing in a breed class can be worth more than a Best In Show if you've really worked on achieving perfection in a particular rat. Above all, don't expect perfection at once—Best In Shows can be elusive. However, no fancier ever forgets his first Best In Show, a real prize to be savoured. Equally important, don't be lulled into a sense of complacency by early successes. I've seen many fanciers achieve top honours very early on in their show careers, often with good stock bought from other fanciers, only to nose-dive as the rats get older and less show-worthy. You need to continue your show success through other rats, by establishing a new line, a new strain—your *own*.

A final word on showing: in any good fancy, peopled by good, honest fanciers, it is not all a terribly deadly serious, cut-throat, win-at-all-costs affair. Nor is it all "just a giggle." It is both serious and fun, in the sense of careful, considered preparation and professional showing of good quality stock, in an atmosphere of convivial good sportsmanship. Go for it! (Further reading: *HOW TO SHOW*, by Nick Mays, published by the National Fancy Rat Society, 1989.)

Breeding

One of the most frequent remarks made by lay-folk about rodents in general and rats in particular is: "I bet they breed a lot." Yes, it is true—the rodent family is very prolific. Being short-lived, the family member species need to reproduce the maximum number of

A successfully handreared litter of rat kittens, five weeks old. A temporary side effect of the handrearing was that the kittens' fur fell out! Happily, they all survived. They regrew their hair and all lived to an average age of two years.

offspring in the shortest possible time, in order that enough of these will survive the many dangers to be found in the wild environment and in turn procreate the species further. Rats are no exception. In the wild state, a doe can rear up to ten litters in a year, each litter containing an average of eight to ten kittens, often more. However, infant mortality is high, so despite the hysterical outcryings of various pundits, there really isn't any threat of us being invaded by rats.

However, in captivity, the reproductive life of fancy rats is, or should be, held in careful check by the rats' owners. There is a great deal more to breeding rats than merely throwing a buck and doe together and letting them get on with it. For instance, what variety is required? As we have just seen, there are many different varieties of fancy rat. If you wanted to breed Silver Fawns, for example,

there is no point in pairing a Silver Fawn with a Siamese, as the resulting litter would be Agoutis. Similarly, with Marked Varieties, it is pointless trying to breed good Hoodeds, with nice, even hoods and straight saddles by mating a Hooded with a Berkshire. Although the genes for both varieties have a common basis, the offspring would be mis-marked. So the whole point of breeding, or more particularly, serious breeding, comes down to two crucial factors: careful pairing on the basis of variety and breeding on the basis of genetics.

Here we hit a point of controversy amongst fanciers from *all* livestock fancies: selective breeding

Opposite page: If you are really intent on breeding rats, you must first devise a sound breeding plan. Take into consideration the well-being of the pair that is to be mated, as well as any future offspring.

A mother rat and her babies. The nest box that you choose should provide protection from drafts.

the other hand, was an Austrian monk who pioneered the science of genetics by experimenting on the cross-pollination of sweet peas and noting the colouration of subsequent generations of flowers (also the texture of the peas themselves). Mendel's detailed notes were not discovered or published until some years after his death, in 1900. Since this time a great deal more work has been carried out by many eminent scientists in the field of genetical science.

What I have said here in very truncated terms does very little justice to the lives and work of these two great men. A far more detailed study of them should be made by anybody wishing to fully comprehend the importance of their work. However, returning to the "Darwinism vs Mendelism" schools of thought in the fancy, the whole "argument" is summed up very succinctly in the words

versus genetics, or, in wider terms, Darwinism versus Mendelism. Charles Darwin was, of course, the noted Victorian naturalist and explorer who, amongst others, expounded the world-shaking theory of evolution, which included the law of survival of the fittest. Gregor Mendel, on

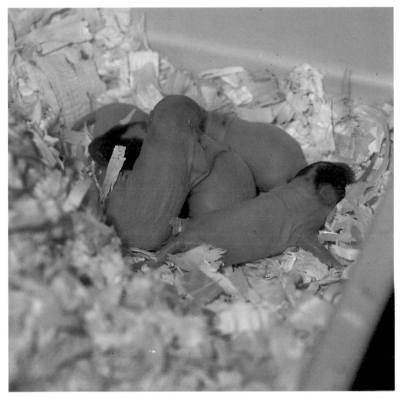

A litter of rat kittens about six days old. At this age, markings are clearly visible. Some of the kittens in this litter are capped.

of Roger Edmondson, one of the most successful and highly respected mouse fanciers of the period from the 1920s to the 1980s. Roger once told me during an interview that "...A geneticist will breed you the right *colour* of an animal, whereas a fancier will breed you the right *shade* of that colour."

The simple fact is, in order to breed good show-worthy rats (or, indeed, just plain, healthy fancy rats), one doesn't need a degree in genetical science. Good husbandry and an eye for a good specimen of a particular breed are the primary requirements. However, a little knowledge of genetics is always helpful, if only to understand why you get such-and-such a colour when you mate this and that variety together.

The rats that you select for your breeding program must be sound, healthy, and of good temperament.

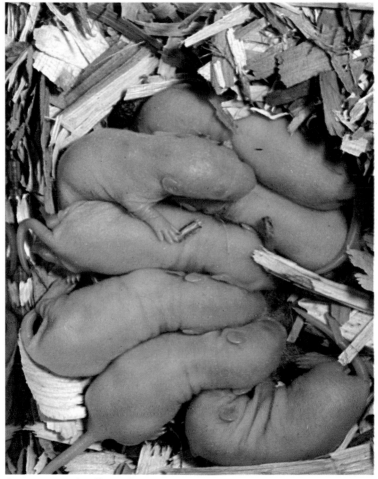

An average-size litter of rat kittens. Rats are born naked, blind, and deaf.

Never select your breeding pair on the basis of appearance only. To do so does not guarantee that the babies will be good specimens.

SELECTING A PAIR

When breeding for exhibition, it isn't as simple as finding two rats, one of each sex, that are good examples of their breed. Just because a rat has a lovely colour or markings does not mean that its offspring will be good examples of the breed. Size and type play as great a part in the selection of an ideal mating pair as colour and markings. Also, as mentioned previously, temperament is a prime requisite amongst the ideal fancy rats. It may sound like a totally fatuous remark to say that bucks and does should be different to each other in appearance. Of course, the obvious difference is that bucks have testicles and does do not. However, the point here is that it should not be possible to confuse a buck and a doe in their type and size.

The ideal stud buck should be solid, but not fat, muscular and heavy, thickset but not with a prominent waist. The buck's head should have a broad skull and blunt nose, well spaced ears and prominent eyes. The back should be arched smoothly, running into a well proportioned tail,

As far as conformation goes, there should be a distinct difference in size between the buck and the doe.

Rats should never be bred before the age of five months as this will be too physically demanding on them.

which should start thick at the base, tapering to a fine, whiplash point.

The ideal doe should conform more to the ideal fancy rat as outlined in the N.F.R.S. general conformation. The doe should be long and racy, but not thin. She should have a long head, but not a sharp muzzle, with well spaced, erect ears, prominent eyes.

The back should be arched smoothly (again, like the buck's), running down the spine to a well-proportioned, whiplash tail. Again, it may seem obvious to state that the better the physical shape of the pair, the better the offspring, but it is a point to keep firmly in mind. Physical faults can "stick" and be inherited. Piggy eyes, small ears, "stick-on" tails—all are very easily inbred into a strain. The optimum breeding age for a doe is between five and ten months. The worst possible factor in bad breeding is breeding purely for colours or markings, without concern for the physical well-being of the offspring. There have been notable cases in past years of extremely inbred strains of rats producing small, weedy offspring, which, although they have lovely colour or whatever, have no physical presence whatsoever. In some cases, inherited physical defects have been observed, such as

A colorful assortment of fancy rats.

taillessness, or even worse, some does being born without vaginas. Also, a number of health problems can be inherited by using poor stock. Don't be misled, however, by the notion that close inbreeding of rats, i.e., brother x sister, father x daughter, can necessarily lead to such defects in offspring. Careful inbreeding can actually improve a strain. So, having selected your pair, taking into account all factors (size, type, colouration/markings and temperament), now is the time to mate them.

MATING

There are two methods of mating the pair (or trio, etc.). The best method for fanciers with large studs is to only mate the rats when the doe is in heat. Does have a five-day oestrus cycle, so basically every five days she will be receptive to a buck. It is usually very simple to spot a doe who is in heat. She will tend to be very jumpy and excitable. If touched on the flanks or towards her rear, she will assume a "frozen" stance and then start to vibrate, particularly from the shoulders up. Sometimes this produces a very comical reaction whereby her ears will, quite literally, "flap," just like wings! Often, a discharge is visible from her vulva. In this case, place the doe and the chosen buck in a "neutral" area, preferably a small cage, such as a show tank or holding box. The buck,

excited by the odour of the doe, will usually mount her immediately. It is best to put a little food in the cage and leave them to their amourous activities overnight, and then split them up the next morning.

The second method is equally simple. Place the buck and doe(s) in a normal-sized cage and leave them together for a week or two, during which time they will probably mate when the doe goes into heat. Sometimes, it takes the pair a few days to "get acquainted," often the two of them sleeping at different ends of the cage. However, love finds a way in the end, and the doe should soon show the primary sign of pregnancy: a distinct swelling of the abdomen, which, when viewed from above, gives the doe an almost pear-shaped appearance. Now they should be split up. If the buck lives alone, no problem. However, if he has come out of a communal

Your rats' accommodations, especially the breeding area, must always be kept clean.

cage of bucks, there is likely to be a great deal of trouble when he is re-introduced. In such an event, he will, to the others, appear to be a stranger to the group, smelling strangely. Fights often occur and can sometimes turn quite nasty. I have found that one possible solution to this problem is to dab a little aftershave or perfume on each buck's belly, which will confuse their own odours and be quite harmless to all concerned. Another method is to thoroughly clean out the communal cage before replacing all the bucks. In any event, you should monitor the situation carefully. If the inevitable sparring goes beyond that into an all-out fight, intervene—carefully! Splashing some water on fighting rats often cools their tempers effectively.

The doe should be removed to a separate cage where she will be able to have her litter. If she goes into heat again, then the

One of the most satisfying aspects of breeding rats is to see the tiny, helpless kittens grow up to be healthy, attractive adult rats.

pregnancy has aborted or
the mating hasn't "taken." If
this is the case, repeat the
mating procedure.

PREGNANCY

Keep the pregnant doe as
quiet as possible during her
pregnancy. The gestation
period is 21-23 days,
although longer pregnancies
can sometimes occur. A few
days before she is due to
give birth, clean her cage
out thoroughly, then give
her plenty of clean shavings
and bedding material. Some
extra food during these last
few days will be most
welcome to the development
of the embryos growing
inside her. Bread and milk
is a useful supplement, and
this is one occasion when
extra protein will not cause
spots.

Usually, the litter is born
during the night. Signs of
imminent birth are that the
doe starts to furiously build
her nest, taking little
interest in her food. A
pinkish discharge will
indicate the beginning of

Hooded rats in a holding cage.

the birth. The doe has a
two-horned uterus, in each
"horn" of which the kittens
are lined up, each within its
own uterine sac. The doe
will squat back on her
haunches, and the kittens

will be born one by one. The doe will bite open the sac around each (if it has not already ruptured) and then nip off the umbilical cord. She washes each kitten to stimulate its breathing and body functions.

The kittens are born naked, bright pink in colour, blind and deaf. They can, however, give high-pitched squeaks so that the doe can locate any of them easily. They quickly seek out her nipples, situated in two rows on her belly, and start to suckle immediately. They receive passive immunity to any infections through anti-bodies in their mother's milk, so, apart from nutrition, this first feed is vitally important. It is easy to see if they have fed, as their stomachs are visible through their skin, showing up as a pale swelling. It is best not to disturb the doe unnecessarily after she has given birth, especially if it is her first litter.

It is very important that the buck has been removed by this stage, as the doe will be sexually receptive to him immediately after giving birth—a condition known as post-partum oestrus. To be pregnant again whilst rearing one litter will present a great physical strain to the doe. Almost certainly the second litter would be very small in size, not having received the full benefit of her bodily nutrition whilst carried during pregnancy. There is some evidence that female rats can, like female rabbits, re-absorb litters if conditions are not favourable for the offspring. Usually, however, if any problems exist, the litter would be born dead, aborted or eaten after birth, as the doe would consider them sickly or even under threat.

The instances of does eating their litters out of fear are relatively small. It is also a fallacy that buck rats will attack and kill kittens,

In the first few weeks after the birth, the mother rat's milk will provide all the nutrients that her kittens need.

or make poor fathers. Whereas the buck, if left with the doe, of course, will stay away from her whilst she is giving birth, he will take his turn in nestling the kittens occasionally, whilst the doe has a break to eat or wash.

There are always exceptions and special circumstances, however, so the best course of action is simply to let the doe get on with rearing the litter with the minimum of interference in the early stages.

RAISING THE LITTER

For the first three weeks of their lives, the kittens are solely dependent on their mother for nutrition. Therefore, it is vitally important to keep the doe well fed. Feed her extra food, with supplements of bread and milk, always ensuring a plentiful supply

Close-up of rat kittens nursing.

At about two weeks of age, the young rats will start to eat solid food.

of fresh drinking water.

If your doe is of a nervous disposition, don't handle the litter in the early stages. However, most rats, being quite trusting of their owners, will allow you to handle their litters almost immediately after birth. Always ensure that you rub your hands in the shavings or bedding beforehand to acquire the "nest smell" and thereby save the doe from getting upset when she inspects her litter after you have handled them. Odd smells can sometimes lead to the doe killing or abandoning some or all of her kittens.

THE CULLING QUESTION

If your doe has had a large litter, i.e., more than twelve (the maximum number of nipples that a doe has), it may be that you will have to consider culling the litter down to a manageable size, for both you and the doe.

I don't propose to launch into a debate on the morals of culling, but there are a few important points to bear in mind on the subject. Firstly, consider the number of offspring that the doe can comfortably cope with. When the kittens become ambulant, the doe often has a great deal of trouble restraining a large number of kittens in the nest. Also, a large litter will jostle for position at the doe's nipples. The stronger kittens will thrive. The weaker ones will not, but may not die, instead growing up as weak and

If the doe has an abnormally large litter, you may be faced with the prospect of having to cull some of the young.

tiny individuals. Remember, the Darwinian law of survival of the fittest doesn't apply so accurately in the domestic situation.

Consider also what you will do with a large litter of kittens after they are weaned. Can you keep them all? If not, will you be able to sell them all? It may well be kindest to prevent them from being unwanted when they are fully conscious and aware of their existence, by putting them to sleep when they are "pinkies" and unaware of their existence. A smaller litter stands a much better chance of developing into large, strong, healthy adults. The best litter size in this respect is four to eight. If you do decide to cull, choose your method carefully. Remember, it must be designed to cause the minimum of suffering to the kittens and must be quick. The most humane method is to place the kittens in a sealed container into which you drop a pad

If a rat is handled from birth, it will be tame and tractable by the time it reaches adulthood.

of cotton wool soaked with ether or chloroform. The kittens will simply drift off to sleep and die quite painlessly. Leave them alone for at least half an hour, then check that all are dead and dispose of the bodies carefully. Ideally, do not cull any kittens until they are four days old. In this way, the doe will have produced milk for a larger litter. With some of the litter culled out, this gives the remaining kittens more milk per kitten.

DEVELOPMENT OF THE LITTER

The kittens in the litter develop rapidly. Their fur begins growing within a day of birth, being more noticeable on kittens who will have dark pigmentation, as these quickly change from a pink colour to a darkish grey. Markings on varieties such as Hooded and Capped will be plainly visible within four or five days, so selection of the best specimens can take place at that time. With lighter and unmarked varieties, such early selection is extremely difficult.

With a little practice, it is possible to sex the kittens within a day or two of birth. The differences are easy to spot. Does have two rows of nipples and the distance between the anus and urethra is noticably closer in does than in bucks.

By the age of ten days, the kittens are fully furred, their ears have opened, and their incisor teeth have broken through. At this stage they will nibble at solid food, which the doe will bring into the nest for them. When their eyes open at fourteen days, the kittens begin to explore the cage and find food for themselves. The doe will often carry any straying kitten back to the nest by the scruff of its neck, just like a female cat will do to her kittens. However, as the kittens grow and become more active, she finds this much more difficult, although they will always find their way back to the nest to suckle. Increase the food quota at this point, to cater for the kittens. Give as broad a mixture as possible, particularly foods with plenty of protein and

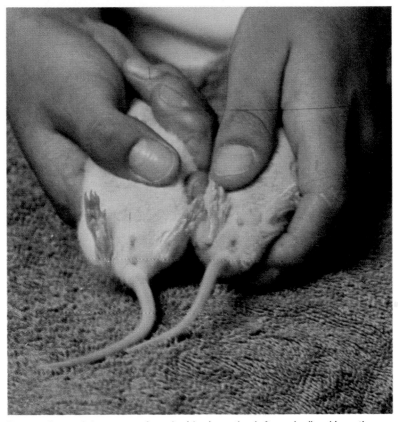

Comparison of the sexes: female (doe) on the left, male (buck) on the right.

fibre, to help build the kittens up. Bread and milk are always nutritious supplements to their main diet and mother's milk.

Healthy kittens will cause you no end of amusement with their playful antics,

If you have plans to breed your female more than once, be sure to give her enough time—about a month—to regain her strength.

chasing each other, wrestling, play-fighting and grooming each other. All this playful activity has a serious side to it, namely the development of a social hierarchy amongst the litter. Some individuals will be more dominant than others, and grooming is a peaceful way of enforcing their dominance over more submissive individuals. Mock mating may also take place, which again acts as a more advanced stage of enforcing social dominance.

As stated, kittens should be handled from birth—doe permitting—and this applies

Rats can reach sexual maturity as early as eight weeks of age.

particularly at this stage of the litter's development. By handling the kittens from a young age, you will teach them not only that humans are not a threat and ensure tameness on their parts, you will also be teaching them that, in the nicest possible way, they, as pets, are submissive to their human owners.

Weaning very much depends on the size of the litter and kittens' development. The very earliest age for weaning is four weeks, but a large litter would still need to suckle to at least six weeks of age, although extra food should be provided to ensure good development. The average weaning age is five weeks, although most fanciers leave their litter with the doe until around six weeks of age, by which time the kittens should be quite capable of fending for themselves.

Sexual maturity can be reached as early as eight weeks of age, so be sure to split the bucks and does up into single-sex groups in suitably sized cages. Provide them with plenty of toys and means of amusement. For a week or so following weaning, bread and milk may be given as a supplement to the standard diet to smooth the transition from mother's milk. Gradually reduce the bread and milk over a few days until cutting it out completely.

Rat kittens should never be weaned earlier than four weeks of age, and it is most advantageous if they remain with their mother until they are six weeks of age.

At six weeks of age, a young rat is fully independent of its mother and capable of caring for itself.

As for the doe, allow her to rest for a day or so after the removal of the litter, then place her back in her usual living quarters. If she has been housed with other does, she will soon be accepted back into the group and a normal routine. Allow her at least two weeks to rest before mating her again, although a "fallow period" of one month would be better.

SELECTING THE BEST FROM THE REST

The earliest age that a rat may be shown is six weeks of age, although in most varieties it is best to wait a few weeks until colour and markings have developed further. Also, and most importantly, the older they are, the better they will be able to take the stress of travelling to a show, let alone taking part. Continue to monitor and select the best specimens for exhibition. Do bear in mind, however, that several varieties, such as Cinnamon Pearl, Agouti and Silver Fawn do not, generally, show well at young ages. Their full coat colour takes some time to fully develop. Most varieties have a drab, greyish tinge to their soft, distinct "baby" coat, until the first moult

A rat is considered an adult when it reaches the age of thirteen weeks. At that time, you will be fully able to assess its overall condition and quality.

takes place between the ages of six and eleven weeks. After this, the final adult coat and colour should be quite clear, if the rat is a good example of its breed. A rat becomes officially adult at thirteen weeks of age. The litter should all have been selected, split up, and housed or sold as required by this time.

The proof of the pudding, it is said, is in the eating. Therefore, if you have selected your breeding pair carefully and correctly, and tended to the resulting litter to the best of your ability, and selected the best kittens, the proof should come with their performance on the show bench, under a good judge. Certainly, don't expect perfection at once. Young rats sometimes don't "show themselves" well until they mature a bit. However, if your chosen kittens are good examples of their breed, then they should start reaping the awards, in

Treat your rat with gentle, loving care and you will have a tame, loveable pet.

which case—aim high—good luck!

If you aren't "into" showing, then raising a litter is a fascinating experience of watching new life develop in its own sake. If you are able to pass the kittens on to good, caring owners, then you, too, have succeeded, by hopefully making some "rat" converts. What could be better than that?

It is not an easy task to handrear orphaned kittens, but your efforts will be more than rewarded as you watch them grow up to become healthy, active adult rats.

HANDREARING A LITTER

As a postscript to the main points of breeding, I have included this section on the handrearing of rat kittens. Having the knowledge of what to do if you have an orphaned litter

As a rat approaches adulthood, its tendency to nibble and gnaw on just about everything will be readily apparent.

on your hands could be extremely useful. Here's the scenario: your doe has had a litter, but for some reason, she neglects them, or perhaps falls ill, or, at worst, she dies. The litter is less than two weeks old and cannot feed or fend for themselves. What can you do? The obvious answer—and what may seem the kindest in many cases—is to cull the litter. But what if this is a special litter? What if you've observed that the kittens have perfect markings as a Hooded or Variegated, perhaps? What if you really need the offspring from a particular pairing? If the doe has died, then that's your final chance to breed from her. Perhaps you are morally opposed to culling. The bottom line is, for one reason or another, you want and need to save the litter, or at least part of it. The best solution is to foster the kittens to another nursing doe, with a litter of a similar age. However, you may not have another nursing doe available, or she may not accept any other kittens. This leaves one option to save your litter: handrearing them yourself.

To start with, remove the kittens to a safe, smaller cage. A plastic fish tank or show tank is ideal. Put soft tissue or a towel or some other form of bedding material on the bottom and place the tank in a warm place, such as on a shelf over a radiator, or in an airing cupboard. The best place is on a heated pad, often used to warm a bed by placing it under the sheets. Alternatively, use an electric blanket. Whatever you do, make sure it is sufficiently warm for the kittens, but not too hot. To gauge this, simply check whether the kittens appear distressed, or too cold, and adjust accordingly.

Next, mix up some milk powder, available from your local pet shop. Follow the instructions on preparation, but be careful to ensure that the mixture is *hand warm,* not hot or cold. The solution must be fed to the kittens from a suitable bottle, which is easier said than done. Try a toy shop, as very small doll's bottles

Opposite page: A Hooded rat in a state of watchful attentiveness.

make ideal feeding bottles for rat kittens (it worked for me!). A small syringe (without needle!) or a pipette will also work.

Now to actually feeding the kittens. They will instinctively know that the bottle spout or teat from which you will be feeding them is not their mother's nipple. In fact, hungry though a kitten may be, it may refuse to feed at first. In this case, you must persevere. Gently hold one kitten at a time and gently brush the "teat" against its mouth until it opens. Put one small drop of milk into the kitten's mouth and wait for it to swallow. *Don't* force the milk down its throat, otherwise it may bubble out of the kitten's nose and suffocate it. This can also happen if the milk goes down the wrong way, so take it slowly and carefully. It may take the kittens a

The author's wife Marianne Mays bottle-feeding an orphaned rat kitten.

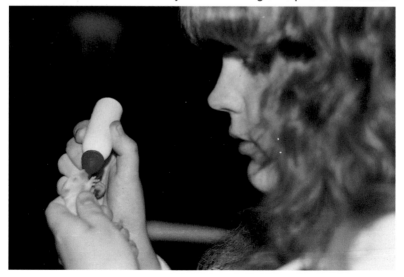

An adult rat that was handreared as a kitten will scurry to the front of its cage if it is approached by a human—especially if it is being offered some goodies.

little while to understand how to feed, but after one or two feeds they will usually learn and actively clamour to be fed, sucking on the teat as well as swallowing. Feed the kittens until you can see their stomachs turning white, through their translucent skin. As they start growing fur, the sign of a full stomach is when the kittens turn their heads away, or even push the bottle away with their paws. It usually takes about five minutes to feed each kitten individually. For the first three to three and a half weeks, they must be fed *every four hours, day and night.* When my wife and I were handrearing a litter of rats, this meant setting our alarm clock as necessary at night, and, on a couple of occasions, taking the kittens (when a bit older) to rat shows with us, to ensure that they were fed on time! So, it can be a bit inconvenient, but if you've had the experience of babies, then you should be used to it. Similarly, once you've handreared a rat litter, then a baby should be relatively easy! Don't be too concerned if the kittens seem to grow a bit thin at first. This is a normal period of adjustment from their mother's natural milk to what you are giving them. They soon start to gain weight and develop normally, although perhaps they remain a little smaller than normal. When they open their eyes, you can

Opposite page: Rats are energetic little animals. They need cage accessories that will keep them occupied.

A really tame rat will enjoy being gently stroked.

the idea and start to eat normally.

At the age of three and a half weeks, cut out the bottle feeding gradually and continue to feed them the rice and milk mixture, mixing this up with various tinned or bottled baby foods (and get used to curious stares from shop assistants in the chemist or supermarket when you start buying the baby foods for babies of different ages!). Feed the kittens three or four meals a day, always making sure to remove any uneaten food from the previous feeds.

Most likely, it will take the kittens a while to learn to wash themselves properly, so you, being their "mother," must wash them, cleaning them up when they get dirty after eating sloppy food. A gentle towelling down with a damp handcloth and drying off with a towel will be fine. Don't be alarmed if their fur begins to drop out when they get especially grubby—this is natural. They may

start to cut down the nightly feeds by increasing the intervals between each feed by half an hour at a time. Now you can start giving them solid food. A milk formula mixed up with baby rice is a good start. If the kittens won't eat it at first, try getting them to lick it off your fingers. They soon get

A well-cared-for rat will be alert and active.

If you do decide to breed your rats, it will be a rewarding and educational project that your whole family can share.

even be temporarily bald, but their fur will grow back eventually, with no ill effects.

At the age of five weeks, house them in an ordinary cage and phase out the milk and baby food mixture, giving them normal rat food instead. Always ensure a broad mixture of diet. The kittens will behave normally, although for a while they may be smaller than other kittens of their own age. With prudent feeding and care, they should develop perfectly normal from here on. One thing is for sure, they will be very tame and friendly, regarding you as their mother. So, hopefully, all the sleepless nights will have paid off, and you will have saved the litter. Handrearing *does* work, so if you manage to get your kittens through it, you've done remarkably well. Seeing a healthy litter at the end of it is worth all the hard work you've put in, so give yourself a pat on the back!

A good illustration of the configuration of a rat's whiskers.

Genetics

Genetics is the science of inheritance and, as such, a fascinating but complex science when viewed in all of its myriad detail. In terms of breeding fancy livestock for exhibition, a knowledge of genetics is not essential, but a little knowledge is always helpful. A brief background in genetics, combined with an eye for good specimens of a particular variety of fancy rat, plus the experience of selecting good, show-worthy stock can be a very useful package, each

Breeding for color can be a complicated matter as some rats do not always breed true.

Familiarity with basic genetic principles can help you to achieve your breeding goals.

Novice fanciers should realize that the breeding of new colors and patterns is not a simple matter.

fancy rat in this chapter, for two reasons. (1) I am not, by any means, an expert in genetics and (2) there are a number of excellent works on rat genetics, written by far more knowledgeable experts than I. So, what follows are the very basics of fancy rat genetics, the tip of a very large iceberg...

WHAT IS GENETICS?

To start with, it may be best to tell you what genetics is *not*, as it is often wrongly and unfairly dismissed by many people. Genetics is not random, hypothetical formulae "invented" to explain inheritance. Genetics is not a form of convoluted mathematics. Genetics is not, like fairies, something you believe or disbelieve in. The science is very real, about very real, living components, which exist in every living organism.

Okay, now I've got down from my soap box and will move on to an explanation of the composite parts of

discipline complementing the others. I do not intend to even attempt to cover the complete genetics of the

the subject. Every living organism is made up of cells. Within each cell are molecules known as *chromosomes*, which form in double-helix spirals, made up of a chemical known as *deoxyribonucleic acid,* thankfully called *DNA* for short. Different organisms have varying numbers of chromosomes within their body cells, but normally in equal number. In the case of rats, this number is forty-two. Genes are short lengths of the DNA spiral. Each particular gene contains

Your rat's genes give the animal a predetermined potential. However, whether or not this potential is fully realized is influenced by two important factors: nutrition and environment.

The success of your line of stock will be governed by the type of animals that you choose to pair.

within it a particular piece of information about the organism—rather like a modern computer file. This information could be structural, physical, or even mental—all combining to form a complete file, or *genome*, of the entire organism.

In order to procreate successfully, animals, including man, produce male and female cells. The female cells are, naturally, produced in the female's body in the form of eggs, whilst the male cells are produced in the male's body, in the form of sperm. When eggs and sperm are produced, each contains exactly half the usual number of chromosomes as

Bad temperament in a rat can be passed on to successive generations. This fact must always be kept in mind when selecting breeding partners—no matter how attractive they are.

are present in normal body cells. In the rat's case, eggs and sperm contain twenty-one chromosomes.

At fertilization, following mating, the sperm fuses with the egg. During this process, the two sets of chromosomes pair up with each other, combining to make forty-two chromosomes. After this, each cell begins to divide into two cells, then multiplies in four, then eigł and so on, doubling constantly, to create the foetus of the new organism... in this case, a rat kitten. The developing

A gene that masks the characteristic of another gene is said to be dominant; the gene that is masked is said to be recessive.

foetus has been "programmed" with genetic information from both parents.

A cell's chromosomes are grouped in pairs, one of each pair coming from each parent. The position that a gene occupies on the chromosome is known as its *locus* (plural: *loci*). On the corresponding chromosome pair, the gene will occupy the same locus. Sometimes, however, a different gene may occupy the loci. The gene will have an effect on the same area as the normal gene, but with different results. This modified gene is known as the *mutant* or *mutant allele.*

Genetics and proper selection are the determining elements in breeding, but good luck occasionally factors in as well.

If a gene's pair of chromosomes each contain the same allele, the gene is termed homozygous. If the alleles are different from each other, the gene is termed heterozygous.

Taking it that, in the normal way, the same gene occupies the same loci on a chromosome, the pairing can take one of two forms. If the other chromosome in a pair contains the same allele as the corresponding chromosome, then the gene is said to be *homozygous*. If the loci on the two chromosomes contain different alleles of the same gene, then the gene is known as *heterozygous*, or recessive. In a heterozygous pairing, one allele will usually be dominant; whilst the other allele will be recessive to a homozygous pairing.

In this case, a recessive factor will be hidden or masked in the rat. For instance, a Black rat can carry the recessive Albino factor, but will physically appear no different than a homozygous Black rat that is not carrying Albino. Both rats will have the same *phenotype*—physical appearance—but will have a different *genotype*—inheritance factor.

CLASSIFICATION

In classifying genetics in written form, it is usual to write a dominant allele with a capital letter and a recessive allele with a small letter, e.g.: CC—full colour, cc—Albino.

Often, more than one

An animal's physical appearance is known as its phenotype; its genetical makeup is known as its genotype.

A fancy rat and a mouse. Note the difference in size between the two.

mutant allele exists, although only two alleles for the same gene can exist in a normal rat. The Siamese and Himalayan varieties are a case in point. In such an instance, the alleles are written in order of dominance. When neither of two paired alleles is fully dominant, this is known as *incomplete dominance*, and both will ultimately have an effect on the rat's appearance.

In this case: CC Full Colour, ChCh Siamese, Ch c Himalayan, cc Albino. There are many different factors to bear in mind in any discipline of genetics, particularly rats. One such factor is that of *polygenes,* a grouping of genes known as *modifying genes* that have minor, but important,

Mutations have contributed to the development of a variety of attractive colors in the fancy rat.

A proper diet will help to keep your stock healthy and looking their best.

effects. Such groups of polygenes control the amount of white in Marked varieties, the level of pigment in Blacks or Minks, and also the level of red colour in Agoutis, Cinnamons and Silver Fawns. This point brings us back to the Darwinism versus Mendelism argument, in a way, as polygenes are more important for the fancier to be aware of, as they actually control the precise variation of colour within a variety. In this way, it may not be simply enough to use major gene pairing to get a good Agouti—the polygenes must be mastered to breed an

When selecting rats for your breeding program, it is advisable to select animals of known ancestry rather than those of undetermined origin.

Polygenes, a group of genes that collectively control the quantitative degree of a given characteristic, are especially significant in the development of color within any given variety.

Agouti that is ruddy enough, as called for in its standard.

RAT LOCI EXPLAINED

At this time, some of the different loci are still being researched and investigated. It is fairly well understood that there are at least seven loci responsible for coat colour and one or two responsible for markings, with one for coat type. The main loci are as follows:

Agouti Locus—A

AA Agouti. Includes varieties: Agouti, Cinnamon, Cinnamon Pearl, Silver Fawn and Topaz (formerly Argente).

In the development of breeding stock, the success of the line highly depends on the breeder consistently making the correct selections from fancy rats that are available to him.

Understanding how heredity works will help to prevent wasted breedings, particularly where easily observed features like color are involved.

aa Non-Agouti. Includes varieties: Black, Dove, Chocolate.

Aa. These rats will display Agouti coat characteristics, just like AA rats.

Brown Locus—B

The Brown locus is still undergoing research. Various theories as to the inclusion of different varieties on this locus have been advanced. As yet, no definite findings have been made.

Albino Locus—C

As mentioned in the example above, the Albino locus gradually reduces from full colour to Albino, via incompletely dominant varieties, the Himalayan and Siamese.

To recap on the codings: CC Full Colour, Ch Ch Siamese, Ch c Himalayan, cc Albino.

Pink Eyed Locus—P

Black eyed rats, PP and Pp, are dominant over pink eyed rats, pp. As well as the effect on eye colouration, pp can also dilute coat colours, such as Black to Champagne, and also slightly reddens the eye pigmentation. Typical pp rats are Silver Fawn and Champagne. Pp rats, a heterozygote, have the same dark eyed appearance as PP rats.

Red Eyed Locus—R

This locus is more common in rats in the United States, the effect of the gene being similar, but not as intense as p. RR Black eyed, rr Ruby Eyed; r reduces Black pigment to a pale Dove grey and Mink to a Champagne kind of colour.

Hooded Locus—H

This locus controls the major form of white spotting on all the Marked varieties of fancy rat. As previously explained, the presence of polygenes makes the classification of the varieties all the more difficult. There are four known alleles: H - Self, hi - Irish, h - Hooded, and h' - patched, although the hi Irish may not exist in the fancy rat and is still the subject of some conjecture.

A Hooded rat. The locus H is responsible for the white spotting.

The six genotypes are: HH Self, Hh Irish/Berkshire, Hh' Variegated, hh hooded, h'h Capped/Patched and h'h' Patched/Black Eyed White.

A minor white spotting gene causes the white spot on the forehead of Berkshires and the blaze on Variegated.

There may well be more genotypes, which would better explain the American varieties *Bareback* (Hooded without a saddle) and *"American Berkshire,"* halfway between normal

Once you have mastered the basics of genetics, you will be able to work out what the possibilities are of obtaining a given color.

Keeping detailed records will be extremely helpful in the development of a given line.

Few features are controlled by a single gene, and color is no exception—many loci are involved.

Berkshire and Variegated. However, many "invented" marked varieties, as they occasionally crop up, have no true genotype. They are examples of bad breeding, pure and simple.

Rex Locus—Re

As yet, Rex is the only coat variant within the rat fancy. It is a dominant gene, producing a short, wavy coat type with reduced, wavy guard hairs, which are allowed for in standards for varieties containing guard hairs (such as Agouti). The curling is particularly noticeable in young kittens and more mature rats over the age of four months. It is less noticeable in between times. Homozygous Rex kittens and young adults tend to go bald temporarily before moulting into a new, wavy coat. All Rexes, however, by the very nature of their coats, have a few bald patches.

There is no separate gene for silvering in rats. All rats are silvered to a greater or lesser extent. Show-quality Silvers are rats that have been selectively bred with this point in mind.

PAIRING

Obviously, with inheritance factors in mind, the establishing of a particular strain may take a generation or two (perhaps longer) to develop sufficiently to reflect the desired traits. In this way, the successive generations from the original pairing are coded as the first, second, third, etc. *filial generation*, abbreviated as F1, F2, F3, and so on.

Here now are some examples of pairing different varieties using a genetical diagram:

Black x Pure Agouti

The genotypes of each are:

AA BB CC DD PP Agouti
aa BB CC DD PP Black

When writing up the formula, we need only concern ourselves with the loci that vary between the two rats, in this case AA

TYPICAL VARIETY GENOTYPES

AA	BB	CC	PP	RR	Agouti
AA	BB	CC	pp	RR	Silver Fawn
aa	BB	CC	PP	RR	Black
aa	BB	CC	pp	RR	Champagne
AA	BB	CC	PP	rr	Topaz (with Dove ticking)
aa	BB	CC	PP	rr	Buff
AA	BB	Ch Ch	PP	RR	Siamese Seal Point
AA	BB	Ch c	PP	RR	Himalayan Seal Point
Any	Any	cc	Any	Any	Albino/Pink Eyed White

and aa. Thus the "equation" runs as follows:

Sire (Agouti)

	A	A
a	Aa	Aa
a	Aa	Aa

Dam (Black)

F1 Generation

All the litter will be heterozygous Agoutis; Aa. If two of the offspring are then paired:

	A	a
A	AA	Aa
a	Aa	aa

F2 Generation

Three out of four kittens will be Agouti and one out of four Black. Obviously, this is only a ratio at 3:1; in a typical litter you would get any number of either. Pairing one of the sons to a Black, for example, its mother:

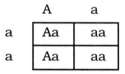

	A	a
a	Aa	aa
a	Aa	aa

This equals a ratio of 50/50. If your object was to breed more Blacks, then this mating is a better one. This method will work for all dominant/recessive relationships at a single locus, and utilises the best aspects of inbreeding. The exception to this rule is when an incomplete dominant is involved, such as Siamese x Pink Eyed White.

Sire (Siamese)

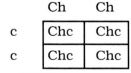

	Ch	Ch
c	Chc	Chc
c	Chc	Chc

Dam (PEW)

All the F1 generation will be Himalayan. When two of the F1s are paired:

Himalayan

	Ch	c
Ch	ChCh	cCh
c	Chc	cc

Himalayan

The ratio is 1 Siamese, 2 Himalayan, 1 PEW—1:2:1.

Of course, matters become far more complex when mating together rats with variations at two, three or more loci. Additionally, factors such as incomplete dominance, polygenes with marked varieties, and Rex genes for coat type make a very, very complex equation indeed. Thus, it is better to read up further on fancy rat genetics if you wish to know more. To attempt to cover such variations would push my page count beyond the publisher's limit! Suffice to say that genetics *is* a useful science to have some knowledge of, particularly if you really want to be sure about your fancy rat breeding programme.

RECOMMENDED FURTHER READING:

Robinson, Roy: *Genetics of the Norway Rat*, pub. Pergamon Press, 1965

Robinson, Roy: *Colour Inheritance In Small Livestock*, pub. Watmoughs Ltd., 1978

Watmough, W: *Practical Inbreeding*, pub. Winckley Publishing, 1955/1988

Storey, Ann: *Genetics* (of Fancy Rats) & *Inbreeding—N.F.R.S. Handbook 1989/91*, also "*Pro-Rat-A*" (*N.F.R.S. Journal*), various issues.

The keeping of fancy rats can be a satisfying and rewarding endeavor—whether you keep just one or two purely as pets, or whether you pursue the show route.

In Conclusion

So, there you have it—the fancy rat. An animal of rare charm, high intelligence and a source of much interest to any owner. Of course, as I've said before, I'm biased in my opinion of fancy rats—I think they're great! So, whether you have decided to keep one or two rats purely as pets, or whether you have opted to build up your stud of future show winners, you have embarked on a most interesting venture—the keeping of fancy rats. In becoming a rat owner, you have, by association, joined what could be termed an elite body: a worldwide fraternity of like-minded, and, by association, open-minded people who have looked beyond the popular myths and misconceptions about the rat and found, in the domesticated rat, an animal worthy of our respect and affection.

It all ties in rather nicely with something that I witnessed just a few years ago, at a rat show where I was judging. The show venue was in a community hall in the middle of a fairly tough North London housing estate, not noted for high standards of cleanliness and general hygiene. Whilst I was in the middle of judging a class, one of our more excitable members dashed in from the kitchen in a state of some anxiety. "Nick! Nick!", she cried, "One of the rats has got out into the garden!" At first, I didn't believe her. All the rats were sitting, quite safely, in their show tanks, awaiting their turn to be judged. Still, she was adamant that there was a rat outside, so, with some degree of resignation, I walked through to the kitchen with her and a few other interested members and looked out of the window into the hall's small, untidy garden area. There, sitting up on its haunches, as bold as brass, in full daylight, was a big, *wild* rat. It was calmly munching away on some pieces of stale bread that somebody had put outside for the birds. Spellbound, we all stared at the rat through the window. The rat, in turn, regarded us calmly, unhurriedly finishing its mouthful. Finally, the last piece of bread eaten, the rat gave itself a quick wash, shook its head and trotted off into the bushes bordering the garden. No doubt he would return to some nest somewhere in a rubbish area in one of the tower blocks making up the estate.

It was the first time that I had seen a live wild rat up close. It was not as attractive as its domesticated descendants in their show tanks in the hall, and I certainly didn't hanker after it as a pet, but I felt within me a great respect, even awe, for this most maligned of species. This wild rat, living in such close proximity with Man, somehow bridged that gap between the perception of wild rats as opposed to fancy rats. Of course, fancy rats are pets, they could not survive in the wild. They are true domesticated versions of a species. The wild rat, however, just proved that, as an entire species, rats are as adaptable and prodigious as Man. In fact, they have existed longer than Man. And, in their own way, they exist alongside mankind. Thanks to the efforts of Jack Black, Jimmy Shaw, Mary Douglas, et al. so many years ago, now we all can experience the intelligence and tenacity of the rat as a pet and as a fine exhibition animal. All that remains for me to say to you now, Dear Reader, as you become a rat owner/fancier is: Good Luck and Happy Ratting!

Index